Other Books by A H Perkins

Category. Children's Mystery / Adventure.

The Lake in Oak wood, ISBN 0-9532563-0-8

The Secret Of Maidwell Bay, ISBN 0-9532563-1-6

Shadows In The Mist, ISBN 0-9532563-2-4

Category. Supernatural Phenomena.

Ghost Detective, ISBN 978-0-9532563-3-4

Ghost Detective II, ISBN 978-0-9532563-4-1

Ghost Detective III, ISBN 978-0-9532563-5-8

All books available through Paris & Wolf Publishing, leading
High Street bookstores and Internet bookstores,
simply quote ISBN numbers.

Published by Paris & Wolf 2008

Acknowledgements

I would like to thank all the people who gave their time
to be interviewed for this book.

With special thanks to,

Tim & Roberta.

David Blagrove.

Angela Brown of Southeast Waterways.

The Northampton Paranormal Group.

All the paranormal investigators, spiritual, and
scientific, who work with me on investigations.

And of course,

BBC Radio Northampton.

Cover photographed by Margaret Needham,

assisted by Charlotte Penny, photographic

H.N.D. Student, Northampton University.

With permission from Abington Park Museum,

Northampton Museum Service.

Contents

GHOST DETECTIVE

III

By
A.H.Perkins.

The Ghost Detective

Dedicated to Denise.

Paris & Wolf
Publishing
June 2008

ISBN 978-0-9532563-5-8

Introduction

In the darkest recesses of the mind lie our deepest fears. Our imagination is capable of conjuring up the most hideous fiends and monsters. Our logical thought processes give way to irrational thoughts and we believe we are in danger, as panic sets in we run to get away from the demons of our mind. Learning to control your imagination is of paramount importance if you wish to search for the paranormal. Removing what your imagination tells you is there, and looking at what is really there can be difficult at the best of times, but once you have mastered it investigating becomes a lot easier. In this book the various teams and myself have investigated Restaurants, Houses, Shops, Museums, even a tunnel on the Grand Union Canal.

The book is not a collection of stories, it is a collection of detailed investigations from the initial interview to the final outcome. We may spend several days on one investigation going back to monitor how things change over time. I say we, over the last two years a group of trusted friends have joined me on investigations, I call them the vigil team. It's not really a team, each person investigates the paranormal in their own way, if they think they need assistance on an investigation they call on one or more of us to help them. It's good to work with people you know and can rely on, and we also have a good deal of fun.

Here is a tip for all you would-be investigators out there. Keep things light hearted, and always try to behave in a professional manner. I am sure if you were to ask any of the vigil team who investigate cases with me, they would probably say I am too laid-back. I like to take a back seat and allow people to do things in their own time. There is nothing wrong with a slow approach; it's very often an advantage.

These are all new stories for the avid paranormal fan and I hope you enjoy reading them as much as we enjoyed investigating them.
Adrian.

La Oficina

It is to the town of Wellingborough, to the East of Northamptonshire, that we make our first call. At the time of this investigation La Oficina was a restaurant that looked out onto Wellingborough's market square. The date the building was constructed is unknown, but it seems to have been part of a larger construction, possibly a warehouse or row of shops. What you see today is the end of the original building and I know through my investigations into the history of Wellingborough that the original buildings were bombed during the Second World War. As you walk around inside the restaurant you can see the different stages of brickwork and repairs that were done before and after the war. Through the years the building has served as many things, from storage house to workshops, printers, nightclub, and restaurant. Why so many things? Well maybe it's the atmosphere that prevails within that caused the changes over the years. It's not an unpleasant atmosphere, just an uneasy one that puts the slightest of thoughts in your mind, is there someone here with me? The answer? Yes there is.

La Oficina Restaurant

The owners of the restaurant at the time of my visits were Judy and Martin Jenner. Hard working people with a friendly smile and welcoming manner. Judy's passion for cooking was evident from the outset, and with a personality and heart of pure gold the customers eating at La Oficina were in good hands. Five star quality food and friendly staff enhancing the experience, so why call me in? Not all ghosts and spirits are frightening, some are inquisitive, while others just plain friendly. In this restaurant we seemed to have the friendly type. I say spirits and not ghosts, what is the difference? A ghost is a recording of a past event played back to you. We all give off energy, and it is this energy that is imprinted in the atmosphere around us. As hard as you might try you will never get a response from a ghost. A spirit on the other hand is the soul of a person no longer in the physical form, and spirits do interact with us. The spirits in La Oficina wanted us to know they were there.

When I first interviewed Judy she told me of activity that was subtle and sporadic. From what she told me I believe some activity was so subtle there were occasions when it probably went unnoticed altogether. Judy was intrigued to learn more about the spirits that inhabited the building, and so was I.

The first vigil we did at the restaurant was on the third of March 2007 and it was a little difficult. The very nature of a busy restaurant is a bustling hive of activity, hardly a place in which to perform a ghost vigil. However, when it comes to investigating all things paranormal, I'm your man.

Judy and Martin, the perfect hosts.

Now to understand how we did the investigations, you need to know the layout of the restaurant and where the rooms were in relation to one another. On entering the establishment from the front you entered into the first of two bars. Walking through the first bar into a small passageway you come across a flight of stairs to your left. These stairs lead to an upper bar and lounge. Back down in the passageway, further along and down to your left is a restaurant; ahead at the end of the passage is a flight of stairs leading down to the kitchen with adjacent garden and toilets. There is also a storage barn attached to the side of the restaurant reached via the garden. Right, now you know your way around you are all set to join us in the first vigil.

The team members on this vigil were, Richard Wright, Judy C, and myself. When conducting an initial investigation it is sometimes better to do it in a small group, concentrate your efforts in one place. We decided to go upstairs to start with, into the lounge bar, Judy had closed this off for us knowing how busy things were. Setting up recording equipment was done in about fifteen minutes and to our surprise Judy, the owner, had laid on some nibbles. We had something to eat and settled ourselves down to start what was the most difficult vigil I have ever done. It took some time to get accustomed to the noises that emanated from downstairs but finally things started to happen around us. It was as though people were waiting for us to become comfortable before trying to communicate with us. Judy picked up on spirits close by and I received the name Elizabeth. Richard was taking photos constantly trying to capture the corner of the eye shadows we were all experiencing. I had the infrared video camera running, you would be surprised what you can pick up with infrared. It's invisible to the human eye but when looked at through the viewfinder, or played back after an investigation, you see things that nobody else can.

I took a shot of something moving by Richard, he was sitting on a black settee in one corner of the room about ten feet away. I was not sure what I had seen at first, just a movement out of the corner of my eye, however when I looked at the picture later I was amazed at what I saw. A bright little orb was floating next to Richard. Not overly exciting I admit, but when you see it has a face, things become a little more interesting.

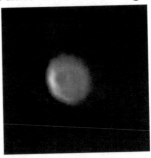

I have seen countless orb pictures, but nothing this well defined. Its size was only that of a fifty pence piece in relation to Richard, and as you can see this picture is blown up quite high, unfortunately the resolution is poor, but look at the light hitting one side. Whatever you believe this is, it's a very interesting object and one we never saw again. From the outset it was clear to all of us we would need to do another vigil through the night at some future date.

I told Judy what we had found and asked her if it would be possible to investigate the building through the night. I explained that the location of the restaurant in relation to the other buildings and businesses around it gave us little or no chance to do an investigation before eleven in the evening. She agreed an overnight vigil was a good idea and a date was fixed. Before leaving we chatted about the work I do and I explained that as well as doing the investigations, I also gave talks about ghosts and spirits. Judy thought it would be a good idea for me to give a talk at the restaurant for charity. There had been a lot of interest in what we were doing and it would give people a chance to ask questions, so I agreed. On the 7th of October I was back at the restaurant talking to a group of paranormal enthusiasts about my investigations and the work we were doing in the rooms around them. After the talk the questions came thick and fast, how do I know if I have seen a ghost or a spirit, how do you know if it is your imagination or a real spirit trying to communicate with you. These were just two from a long list of good questions asked that night. The paranormal fascinates people worldwide. Not only do we wish to know our heritage, it's the future people need to know about. The belief in an afterlife gives us a sense of security and comfort. If you are now wondering about the answers for the two questions that were asked, here they are. How do I know if I have seen a ghost or spirit? A ghost is simply a recording imprinted in the atmosphere around us, you cannot interact with a recording. On the other hand a spirit will interact with you by touching you or talking to you, it will acknowledge you in some way. The second question was how do you know if it is your imagination or a real spirit trying to contact you? If the information you receive can be verified, and you had no prior knowledge of the information then this is not imagination, it's spirit. My wife Denise accompanies me when I give talks even

11

though she has heard it all a thousand times before. The support she gives is a tremendous help to me. Denise sells copies of my books while I answer questions after the talk has ended. All in all the evening talk at La Oficina was a success, and we also raised some money for charity.

La Oficina Vigil two

20/4/07 10.30 p m start till 3.30 am.

Attending this vigil would be Judy C, Richard Wright, Adam Faulkner and myself. We started the evening investigation with a circle. For people who have not experienced a circle let me explain what it is and what its aims are. Circles are performed with a group of people wishing to contact the spirits of the departed. It's a way of combining a collective energy field helping the spirits link with us. From a personal viewpoint the meditation and relaxation required to assist in a circle can take some time to master. However, a successful circle can be a valuable aid when investigating haunting's of any type.

The dining area at La Oficina
where the circles were held.

12

La Oficina's restaurant area was the perfect place for the circle, at the start I said I was not really expecting much to happen, big mistake, I should have known better. Seconds after saying this came a loud knocking on a door about six feet from us, as though someone wish to enter. The door is in fact an internal door leading to a storage room, there was no one in there. A tingle swept down my spine as I looked across at Judy, she was shaking her head and smiling. Adam started to laugh and said, I think we are in for a good night. The anticipation of the group had just hit the roof. Richard, as always, went walkabout with the night vision camera. This was one occasion when a circle would be done later if needed. We all moved to the stairwell that leads down to the kitchen and garden courtyard, this is not a place you would linger for long if you were alone.

Stairwell leading to to the kitchen and garden

Once again we heard thuds and bangs from inner walls, tentatively we moved down to the basement where I saw a figure standing in the kitchen doorway. I estimated the figure to be at least six foot tall and possibly the figure of a man, but could not say for certain as the sighting only lasted for three or four seconds. We formed a circle in the kitchen to try to communicate with whoever it was. This resulted in a loud metallic bang on the floor, as though

13

something had been thrown, we later found a hook from the overhead pan rack had fallen, or been thrown to the floor.

Other phenomena in the kitchen came in the form of cold drafts when standing with your back to the far wall. Interestingly, Judy had seen a picture in her mind of how the kitchen once was, not as a kitchen, but as a room that extended through what is now the back wall and continued for some distance. The existing wall was once an archway leading into this extended room where there were machines for leather or wood working. At one point the centre island in the kitchen shook violently as if being hit with some force. The names Peter Taylor, and a boy of six or seven called Adam came to the fore, also Clarence, a man with leg problems, and a woman identifying herself as Gladys. In my mind I saw images of bomb damage buildings and a sign on one of the buildings with a name beginning with a B and ending in "And Sons". I had the feeling the area had been bombed and that seven people died, one of these being a small child. Later through research we found this to be accurate. Richard took some fantastic photos of ghosts, one appeared to show a spirit superimposed with me.

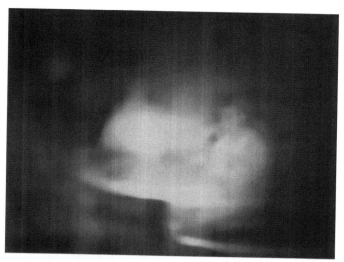

This photo appears to show a spirit sitting between Judy and Adam, this is one of the eeriest shots I have ever seen. People often say we read into photos what we want to see, especially if the picture is a little obscure. The problem is, if you are showing a photo to a non believer, you will never convince them it is genuine. Even a photo of a full size apparition as fully formed as you or I will still not convince them. It's a mind-set that you will never overcome, and one you should not waste your energy trying to. The activity during this second vigil at La Oficina was remarkable, a few days later we would learn the true significance of the names we had been given. The reason why the owners of the restaurant, Judy and Martin had not attended the vigil was they were due to fly off on holiday the following day. However, Judy could not find her passport, and the holiday was postponed.

Unknown to us at the time Judy, in pure frustration, had asked the spirit of her late father to help her search for the passport, her fathers name was Clarence. Was it Judy's father who was trying to get a message to her regarding the passport? We knew we would be back at La Oficina for another vigil, and this time it would be with a full team. The information we were receiving was beginning to make sense and a picture of why the restaurant is haunted was now appearing. There are spirits within the building who worked and spent a good deal of their lives there. They simply like to drop in and watch people. The sounds are mainly from ghosts, recordings of past events replayed over and over again. Remember, spirits are spiritual, and ghosts are a natural phenomenon, they must be kept separate from each other. Only sounds that answer your questions with banging or words can be linked with spirit.

Vigil three La Oficina 22nd of June 9.00 p m

Team members for this vigil were, Judy C, Adam Faulkner, Mark Adams, Richard Wright, Andy Ellis and myself.

On arriving at La Oficina for our third vigil it was clear the team were in an excited mood, with the energy levels this high it was going to be a good vigil. Judy and myself were the last to arrive, and I must admit I felt a little too relaxed to start a vigil. Some people like to sit and relax with meditation before trying to contact the spirit world, Judy C is a great advocate of this method and it works for most people. Personally I like to have the adrenalin running and feel the energy from within. Before the vigil started we all stood in the bar talking for a while. You should always try to incorporate a social side to investigations, after all it may have been some time since you last saw one another, and it may be a while before you see one another again. I also like to chat with the client and find out where the latest activity is centred. Judy, the owner, explained that during one night the previous week, flowers had been strewn across the floor from a vase standing in an old fire place, and the vase was still upright in its correct position. Judy and Martin were not staying for the vigil and so handed the keys over to Adam and said their goodbye's. I had tried to persuade Judy to stay but to no avail, this was a shame because I am sure with her present during the investigation things would have been even more productive. A plan of action was outlined, then completely ignored, you should always go with your instinct wherever it may lead you. We started the vigil with a circle, hoping this would trigger a

16

response, however, what we received was a flood of information. It was not as people often think, coming through people with trained mediumistic powers. It was concentrated information given through people with open minds and a willingness to accept that the information they were receiving was correct. It is a misconception that only people with special powers can receive information from the spirit world. With practice we can all do it, you just need to be dedicated enough to stick at it.

Where was I? Oh yes! The information being received was very detailed, names, dates, and professions. Here is a list of just some of the names and dates.

The name, Charlie Fletcher Cooper, or a Cooper by trade? Had something to do with a fire in 1749.

Cabinet makers in 1790 Joseph Parker.

The feeling of another fire around that time. Shop closed in 1958?

Other names were, Thomas & May Clarke, 1840.

Raymond Harris, 1840.

Clarence, man in light suit and red tie.

Ron Turner.

A child by the name of Raymond Cox, 8 to 12 years.

Alex Rathbone or Rathborne, 1845.

St Martins, Kitchen shop?

Johnny Williams, 3 years old.

Adam, 6 to 8 years old 1871 / 72.

Jack Digby, 1940.

Clarence Hudson.

Also a woman called Violet worked here.

Now you would think with all this information it would be a simple task to track these people down. Wrong. Near on impossible. Maybe someone reading this book will recognise a name associated with this building and contact me. I do hope so.

After the circle was over we decided to split into two groups. One group would stay in the restaurants kitchen area, group 'A', while the other group 'B', would go into the storage barn linked to the side of the building, this experiment would prove extremely

17

enlightening. In group 'A' were Judy, Adam, and myself, in group 'B' were Richard, Andy, and Mark. For our group in the kitchen area it became a spiritual session very quickly, starting with sounds of shuffling movements in the darkness. Unnerved, Judy and Adam started picking up on a female spirit who seemed to want to help me. At the time I was suffering from chronic back pain, and had done so for some time. I remember feeling someone standing close by my side and at that very moment Adam said the spirit was very close to me. I should have asked in which sense he meant close. I knew Judy and Adam were both standing on the opposite side of the kitchen due to the direction of their voices, a flash from my camera confirmed this. What happened next I still think about from time to time. I felt an arm move across my back and onto the area of the pain. I felt a few seconds of heat and the pain in my back eased considerably, it did not go away but it was much easier than before. Adam said the spirit knew I was in pain and just wanted to help me. I thanked the female spirit for her help and Judy said she sensed the spirit moving away. Judy has always said that spirits are often here to help us through our darkest hours. I think she knows more about the spirit world than many so called experts . She has studied spiritualism at length and has a wealth of knowledge on the subject, a good person to have on your side when things go a little over the top. I was also very impressed with Adam, he has strong spiritual abilities considering this was only his second investigation. In my experience, people investigating haunting's become more sensitive to the spirit world the longer they are in close contact with it. Whether this is due to their spiritual awareness growing, or simply to them being in the right place at the right time, I don't know. Whatever the reason is, an experienced group of people can do far more than a group of novices.

Meanwhile, back in the storage barn, things were starting to make sense. One or two people in group 'B' were picking up on the workshops that we believe had once operated in that part of the building during its long history. The names we had discovered earlier also seem to be linked to this area. Again the smell of burning timber was experienced by the entire group, there must have been a fire in this building somewhere in its history. As the two groups swapped locations you could tell each of us was itching to tell the other about what had been experienced. We do not have many rules on our vigils, but one is paramount, never discuss what you have experienced in a location until all who are present have been to all locations. Enthusiasm allows for, thumbs up, saying "You are going to love that one", or even, " You are not going to believe that place", but try to refrain from a full detailed discussion about a location. The credibility of a paranormal experience is vital, if you have more than one person seeing or hearing something you can validate it, it then becomes a credible piece of evidence that is hard to dispute. If you tell someone you saw something in a corner, or by a window, then they say they saw it afterward the credibility has gone.

The swap over complete, it was our turn to experience the storage/workshop barn. It was a surprisingly long building accessed gained at one end via a flight of stairs from the garden area. On entering the barn you could see at the far end the connecting door to the restaurant. The roofing timbers were identical in construction to that of the restaurant, not surprising I suppose due to the fact it is part of the same building. But unlike the restaurant this area has had half its beams lofted out for extra storage. It makes sense when you think of the place as a workshop, it would be an ideal place for storing stock parts. After an initial explore we settled ourselves down and I switched out the lights. It's surprising how the darkness concentrates the senses and allows you to detect things. The smell of burning wood was something we all experienced, as was a strong feeling of pride, seemingly connected to someone working with his hands, a craftsman of some kind in wood or leather. There were other emotions felt, guilt and desperation, the latter linked to the place closing down. The names and dates we had received earlier made more sense now, this place had indeed been a workshop for people and trades over the years. It is a mix of the energy left by peoples emotions, and the recorded smells and sounds that we were getting in the barn, not spiritual as in the restaurant. Our time in the location was up and we made our way back to the main building where the nights findings would finally be discussed. The similarities in the two groups findings were remarkable, sounds, smells, and feelings, had been experienced by almost all of us. I would say that about seventy percent of the nights findings were verified. Obviously a percentage is down to a persons own thoughts and imagination, I accept and expect this each time we go out on a vigil. If I said one hundred percent of what we come up with is correct it would be a lie. People are not infallible, our thoughts and emotions change depending on the environment in which we find ourselves at any given time. It's the information we receive that can be verified by independent sources, and that we had no prior knowledge of, that is real spiritual contact.

On the 22nd of February 2008 we investigated La Oficina for the last time. The people attending this investigation were, Richard, Lewis, and myself. Guests were Alice and her daughter, who held the keys for the owner, and three students from Northampton University studying TV and film production. They had asked to film a documentary about me at the time, and this would be an ideal opportunity for them to gain experience using night vision cameras. We started the vigil at 10.00 pm and planned to finish at 3.00 am, this would give us time to do the investigation, and allow the documentary lads sufficient time to do their filming and interviews.

I spent a little time bringing people up to speed about recent activity within the property. This done Lewis went around each room taking EMF, RF, and temperature readings. This was one of the smallest and shortest investigations we had ever done and there were more cameras and sound recording equipment than we had ever had on an investigation Alice and her daughter would join us, and take an active part in the nights proceedings.

This investigation would prove to be difficult due to the increased noise emanating from the nightclub close by. I have never backed away from a challenge and I wasn't about to start now. Lewis had recorded a humidity level upstairs of 71%. Now considering the property had been empty for several days with the heating off we found this humidity reading rather unusual, and high humidity can cause orbs on photographs. There had been, in the past, incidents of video cameras being hit or switched off during the vigils, something people needed to be aware of. Lewis also bought our attention to the noise levels coming from the club, these can carry infra sound that can affect a persons emotions. I set up the infrared camera at the bottom of the stairs in the kitchen area, the camera would point up the stairs where footsteps had been heard on previous vigils.

We were set up and ready within an hour of arriving so it was time to go to night vision and start the investigation. Richard sat in a far corner of the restaurant by an emergency exit, was he keeping something from us? Lewis was monitoring things from the corner to Richards left. Alice and her daughter sat at the table to my left, and the students completed the circle. I asked the people around the table to sit and relax for a few minutes before we tried to communicate with any spirits. None of the people had been in a circle before so I needed to do things calmly and slowly. You would be surprised just how much your heart rate can climb when doing your first vigil. When I was sure people were settled I began to ask out. Interestingly after asking Richard if he could sense anything there were two distinct clicks, or taps, from somewhere in the room. I then asked each person around the table to ask if there were any spirits present with us. I had the recorder running all the time so I could check for EVP's later. Sometimes the spirits select one person within a group and will communicate to them alone. Richard photographed a large red orb, a type I had never seen before, and it was Richard who had the first of the nights activity. He had his trouser legs tugged at shortly after we had asked for the spirit of Adam to come forward. Adam is the spirit of a small boy we had communicated with on earlier vigils, and he likes to tug at your clothing. Richard also said his legs were extremely cold. At that point Alice and myself felt an extremely cold rush of air hit us, on my left and her right side. Richard then experienced tingling in one of his legs. We were not sure if this was due to the cold temperature or paranormal activity. To be sure, Steve, one of the students volunteered to swap places with Richard to see if he would experience similar events. Interestingly he reported feeling colder sitting in the corner than he did sitting around the table, but the laser thermometer indicated he was three degrees warmer. Then Lewis said he was getting the feeling someone was behind him, he said the feeling was so strong he actually wanted to turn to see if anyone was there, and for Lewis to say that, believe me that's rare. Alice explained that this feeling is common to all the staff while working here. We decided to stop the circle and split into two groups and relocate to other rooms in the restaurant. Our group decided to continue trying to get responses to questions in the main restaurant area. Lewis said he heard something move against the door next to him. There was then a sigh heard in the area between Alice and myself, her daughter then said she saw a dark shadow move by the mirror next to the entrance. Steve, still siting in the corner, thought he felt tugging on his jeans. He then saw movement in the entranceway but couldn't identify what it was. Shortly after that he had a major tug on his right leg. He was convinced there was something, or someone in the corner with him. After a while things became notably quieter. Lewis went upstairs to check on the equipment and Richard went downstairs into the kitchen. Things remained quiet so it was decided to have a break and something to drink.

On resuming we split into smaller groups and Alice had an excellent idea, as we seemed to be getting activity when asking the little boy to contact us, she thought it would be a good idea to give him something to play with. She took some drinking straws downstairs and asked Adam to come and play, and at that point they heard footsteps close to them. I was upstairs chatting to Lewis when we heard something click in the corner. Investigating this we found a beaded curtain moving as if someone had touched it, or brushed by it. As it seemed to be getting lively again I thought it was time to do a solo vigil down in the kitchen area. Lewis said he would place a lock off camera in there with me to monitor any activity that happened, sounded like a good idea to me. Being left alone in the kitchen was interesting to say the least. It wasn't dark, the neon flycatcher on the wall gave out a moonlight type light which reflected in the stainless steel work units. After a time my eyes became accustomed to the light and it was quite pleasant down there. I asked out several times and heard tapping against a small door to my right. I pushed against the door to see if a draught could have moved it, but it was solidly closed and would not give at all. There was then a flash of bluish light behind the camera that Lewis had placed in there with me. A few moment later I heard people coming down the stairs, the door opened and Lewis came in and said we had the keys to the outbuildings and they were all off to explore them. I told him about the flash of light and he checked his camera. I decided to join the group exploring the outbuildings. Lewis said that his camera from the kitchen had recorded nothing at all, although he had checked and made sure it was working as he left me, he couldn't understand what had happened.

One of the outbuildings attached to the restaurant.
In the picture above, the far wall has a bricked up door and archway which at one time would have lead to the main part of the

23

restaurant. On previous investigations we have done, there had been knocking on the door which still remains in place on the other side of the wall.

The whole group were now assembled in the upper room of the outbuildings. I could smell leather quite clearly and others could smell fresh cut wood. It was nice to see people's senses were at a high level of awareness and they were all blocking things out. There was no spirit contact in the buildings, but the atmosphere was electric. Studying the brickwork it seems the building had at one time been used as a workshop. You could see where a long workbench had been positioned against one wall. A door high up in an outer wall had a pulley attached above it, obviously to bring goods into the upper buildings. You can learn a lot by simply looking at a building.

Back to the investigation. We regrouped in the restaurant dining area, Richard, Alice and her daughter decided to go down into the kitchen to do a vigil. Lewis, the students, and myself went upstairs to the upper lounge bar to try a vigil there. On entering the lounge bar it was clear things were not going to be any easier up there. The noise from the club close by was so loud we could hear conversations of people congregating outside smoking. Lewis did record a high humidity level of above 70%, but the room itself was extremely cold. After about twenty minutes in there we had definitely had enough and made our way downstairs to see if Richard and Alice had faired any better. They had much better luck than us and were feeling very pleased with themselves. They had been asking out and had heard shuffling and knocking from just outside the kitchen door. Now it has to be pointed out at this point that this area has been noted by mediums with us on previous investigations. It seems the area around the kitchen and toilets was once a walkway or thoroughfare, activity here seems to be high.

At 1.00 am the club close by closed and things were a little quieter. Steve decided, quite bravely, to do a solo vigil in the kitchen and record the event. The rest of us stayed in the dining area to do some filming and asking out. Unknown to Steve we asked the spirits to make contact with him on his lone vigil. After we had been asking out for a little while we heard what sounded like pots and pans clashing together down in the kitchen. Whether Steve had hit the pans accidentally we would have to wait to find out. We had partially closed the doors to the dining area before starting our vigil. Lewis thought he could see the door moving back and forth. Richard said the doors were quite sturdy and needed some force to move so it could not be due to draught. Our humidity levels were now up to 82% so I took a shot to see if I would capture any orbs. Sure enough the high humidity caused orbs on the photo. When Steve emerged from his vigil he reported photographing two orbs, one on still camera and one he saw on video camera travel from the floor to the ceiling. We asked him about the sound of pots and pans clashing together and he said he heard walking about where we were and this had caused the pans to hit each other. Interestingly though, we were all seated when we heard the sounds in the kitchen.

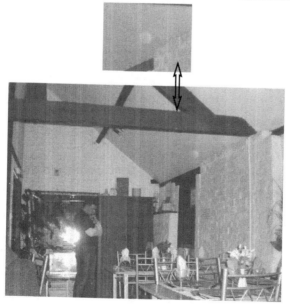

An orb captured while humidity levels were high .

All too soon our time was up at the restaurant and it was time to collect the equipment together. I thanked Alice for her help with the

25

investigation, and the students for joining us. Overall the investigation proved quiet, but still interesting. There had been things seen, heard and felt that we could not explain through normal means. When reviewing the sound recordings I had three EVP's from the later part of the night that sounded like voices very close to the recorder. Again the EVP's came over the top of people talking, a pattern I have recognised in the past.

La Oficina is haunted by spirits, and holds the memories of many ghosts. None of the spirits there are in any way evil or cold hearted. Indeed the spirits that do dwell within its walls are kind hearted and caring souls that seem to be interested in what people are doing, more than trying to be heard themselves. I like the place, the people, and the spirits there. I hope one day soon I will return to a restaurant I consider to be one in a million.

Blisworth Tunnel

During another stint on BBC Radio Northampton, a listener phoned in to ask if I knew Blisworth Tunnel was haunted. I replied that I was not aware of any reports of ghosts being seen there, even though it is an atmospheric place. The tunnel itself is situated between the villages of Stoke Bruerne and Blisworth, on a stretch of the Grand Union Canal in Northamptonshire. Stoke Bruerne is also the location for the British Waterways Museum. Now explaining to people that Blisworth Tunnel is probably one of the most difficult places to attempt a vigil, and to explain this on the radio, I should have known better. But I wasn't kidding, it is possibly the most technically difficult place to do an investigation, paranormal or otherwise. Fortunately for me the radio interview was being listened to by somebody who not only had an interest in the paranormal, but who could also help with the logistics of such an investigation.

Tim & Roberta live on a fifty foot narrow boat on the river Nene close to Northampton . It was Tim who had been listening to the radio interview, and who thought he may be able to help me. He contacted the radio station while we were still on air to offer his services. I said I would contact him after the show to discuss the project. Later Tim told me after he had telephoned the station he returned home to announce to his wife Roberta, that he had offered their home to a ghost detective to conduct an investigation through Blisworth tunnel, and he survived to tell the tale. Top man.

A day later I rang Tim and laid out what I proposed to do. Tim listened quietly, and once I had finished he told me the regulations he has to abide by, and permissions I would need to obtain, in order to do such an investigation. I wanted to do this properly and he listened careful to everything said, writing a list of things as he spoke. He said if I could get the written permission, and abide by all the safety regulations, then we were in business. There was a lot more to this investigation than the actual trip through the tunnel. I had to decide who would be on the boat, and what equipment we would be using. Tim had already set the number of people he was comfortable with on the boat to nine. Out of this number I had decided to have five people doing the investigation, Tim and Roberta made seven, and this left two places for extra people. I needed to speak to someone regarding the waterways regulations. I would also need permission from them to do a midnight run through the tunnel, without permission there would be no investigation.

It was to Angela Brown of Southeast Waterways that I turned for advice, she was intrigued by the proposal. The investigation through the near two-mile long canal tunnel would be possible, if we met certain requirements, official permission would then be granted. After some back and forth conversations over several weeks all parties were eventually happy and a date of the fifteenth of June was set. Angela wanted to put a representative from British Waterways on board to help us, both Tim and myself were in full agreement to this. The last place on the investigation was reserved for a reporter from a local Northamptonshire newspaper, or radio, should they wish to cover the event.

I asked all people concerned with this investigation to keep it quiet. If there is one thing that is sure to bring out the idiots and mischief makers it's a publicized paranormal event. British Waterways thought publicity could be arranged, but did understand my concerns. It was agreed to give the investigation publicity after the event.

As the date grew closer the weather took a turn for the worse. Now considering Tim and Roberta live on the river, things were getting a little bit worrying for them. A week before the investigation Tim rang and said that they were stuck at their moorings unable to move. The heavy rain had caused the river to swell considerably and it was far to dangerous for them to even attempt to move. Even if the rain stopped now it was going to be touch and go for them to reach the tunnel on time. I asked Tim to keep me posted and wished him all the best. The investigation was now at the mercy of the British summer, I wasn't very optimistic.

Tim rang a few days later, he was at Blisworth and the investigation was on.

Sounds good at the moment doesn't it. But nothing runs according to plan and I should have known better.

No media reporters could attend, one of the investigation team dropped out, and British Waterways were unable to attend. All this on the day of the investigation.

Luckily a replacement was found for the team at the last minute and I decided to add one more person to help. Angela Brown emailed the written permission for the investigation to me, without it we could not start.

At last all was set. We met by the boat at the Blisworth entrance to the tunnel, it was 6.30pm Friday the 15th of June. After a talk from Tim pointing out safety procedures in the event of things going wrong, we were ready to set up for the investigation.

The 50ft narrow boat was a snug fit for the seven of us, but we managed to sort out who would be where with what equipment relatively easily. Up front, and inside, were Richard, Ken, Lisa and

Roberta. To the rear by the tiller of the boat were, Tim, Judy and myself, exposed to the elements. It has to be remembered at this point that, (INCHY) the boat, was somebody's home, and as such Tim and Roberta had the right to stop the investigation at any point. The truth was I think they were as excited as the rest of us to see what would happen, and it's true to say we all gelled almost immediately.

From left to right
Lisa, Judy, myself, Ken, Tim, Roberta, Richard,
and Lady, the camera shy dog.

During the initial run through it became clear very quickly that the positioning of people was right. All night vision camera work, and still photography would be shot from the front of the boat. The paranormal side of the investigation would be carried out from the stern, with Judy, Tim and myself. I tried to do some night vision video work from the stern but it was impossible so I decided not to persist with it. I could do one or two still shots from the stern and also do the sound recording from there, but from the first run it was clear we would have our hands full with paranormal contact, now that surprised me. What was also a surprise, to all of us, was the amount of water raining in through the tunnel roof. Tim gave Judy and myself warning of approaching water cascades, this gave us time to cover up camera, sound recording equipment, and ourselves.

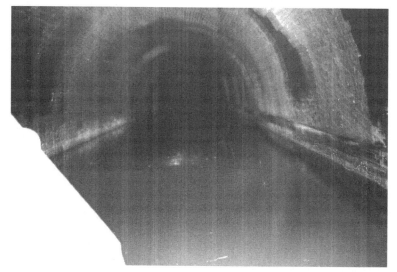

The daunting view of the tunnel as water cascades down.

There had been a few days of heavy rain prior to this investigation and the water was still draining through the soil above the tunnel.

At this point I must stress that only Tim had any prior knowledge of the history surrounding Blisworth Tunnel, and he wasn't going to let us know anything until after the investigation had ended.

After the first run I knew something was going to happen. It's a feeling I have had many times in the past and it has never let me down.

On the first run the atmosphere in the middle part of the tunnel was different, we had also experienced the strange smell of a coal fire, similar to that of a steam rally.

Now all the equipment was set we were ready to start the midnight run. No boats had been through the tunnel for hours so we knew it was clear of fumes. Tim checked the boats electrical systems in case we experienced any power drain, all checked out fine. The cameras started to record as we drifted into the tunnel.

Entering Blisworth Tunnel from the Stoke Bruerne side at Midnight this bright orb was photographed.

The low rhythmical drone from the engine and the sound of water dripping into the canal from the roof above our heads set the scene. As we made our way slowly forward into the tunnel you could sense the feeling of anticipation from all on board It was a good way into the tunnel when the first names came to me. It's like remembering something from the past, you tune into the energy left by events long ago. I picked up on two names, Bill and Edward. Bill, or William, was the younger of the two. I felt as though he had been a local man and he had something to do with wood. Edward was older and harder to identify properly. I felt both men died together in this tunnel, and slowly. I also picked up on two boats, but couldn't get names for them.

By now Judy, Tim, and myself, were experiencing a very strong smell of coal fire fumes. We knew it wasn't our boat and there was nothing else to be seen in the tunnel. I then got a surname of Webb, which I think was Billy's but couldn't be sure, and the years 1860 and 61. Judy then began to pick up on an accident, a cave-in where a number of men had died. She also got the names, Goldsmith and Anthony Wheritt. Goldsmith had a feeling of pride with him, and Wheritt seemed to be a worker. Judy also picked up on a member of Tim's family who she described and he identified, this spirit was standing with us at the rear of the boat. At the same time that we were picking up on these individuals, the people at the front of the boat were getting some strange still shots on camera.

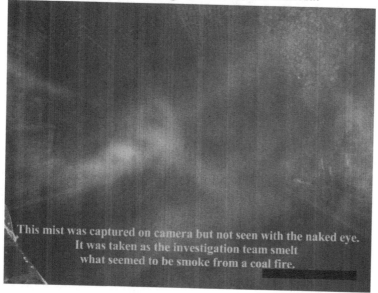

This mist was captured on camera but not seen with the naked eye. It was taken as the investigation team smelt what seemed to be smoke from a coal fire.

Strange orbs and mists were being photographed. Lisa, Richard, and Ken were all getting some good still shots.

Judy felt someone was standing, or sitting, on the ledge in the tunnel as we drifted by, Tim and myself also had identical feelings but could see nothing.

We drifted past the half way point and waited to see what else would happen.

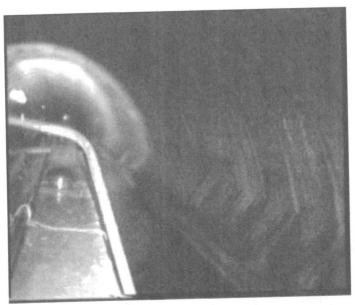

Sure enough Judy began to pick up on a baby being lost. It was a strong feeling, and towards the Blisworth end of the tunnel it grew much stronger. It seemed people were looking for the child but without success. She also got the name of a company Hicks & Co.

All too soon the trip through the tunnel was over and we sat and chatted over what we had experienced. Tim then told us what he knew of the history of the tunnel. Judy was spot on with her cave-in and the name Goldsmith, and the baby being lost. There were leggers that had died from smoke fumes and these could have been the men I had picked up on.

It has to be said, the people picked to do this investigation were the right ones. I am fortunate enough to know many paranormal investigators and mediums, and this is useful when planning vigils. Each member of a team brings their own unique approach to a given situation. This approach means each investigation is fresh, and you avoid the personality conflicts many paranormal teams suffer from.

My thanks to Tim and Roberta, for their hospitality and patience, I count them as true friends. I now needed to do some more research into the names of the people mentioned. This was the paranormal side of the investigation done, now I will investigate the facts and see if we get a match.

Our little investigation had caused quite a stir within the festival at Stoke Bruerne. I was contacted by Roger Hasdell, editor, publicity officer, and archivist for the Northampton branch of the Inland Waterways Association newsletter, Endeavour. He asked me if I would write a piece for the newsletter about the investigation we had just done. I agreed and asked him if he knew of anyone who could tell me about the history of the Tunnel. Roger said the best person to help me was David Blagrove, local writer and historian, he knows all there is to know about the tunnel.

The following day I rang David Blagrove and arranged to meet him regarding the history of the tunnel, the second part of the investigation was now underway.

I began the meeting by telling David what we had done regarding the investigation through the tunnel, and asked him if he could verify any of the names or dates we had come up with. David listened carefully and asked if we had noticed the marker points inside the tunnel. These were important as they were distance markers that had been put in the tunnel during repair work in the eighties. Unfortunately, although we had seen them, we had taken little notice of them. David explained that if we had known exactly were we were when picking up on things, it would be easier to verify. However, the team had taken pictures of the tunnel where the paranormal activity had occurred, this would prove invaluable later. David then went on to explain what he knew about the tunnels history.

On the 6th of September 1861 there had been a bad accident in the tunnel with a steamboat. On board the boat were, William Gower, Joseph Jones, (Engine driver and engineers), they called them engine drivers in those days as they were responsible for the maintenance and good order of the steam engine. Others on board were, Edward Broadbent, (Captain), and William Webb, (Carpenter). It was Edward Broadbent and William Webb that had died in the accident.

Steam had only just been introduced onto the canals and they hadn't fitted out boats for commercial work until the 1860's, so these boats were still in the experimental stage. The Bee, a boat owned by the Grand Junction Company, was heading south from Birmingham towards London. The boat developed trouble just after Long Buckby, about fifteen miles from Stoke Bruerne. The fault seemed to be caused by sooty boiler tubes, these should been cleaned on a regular basis and probably hadn't. They were also burning a type of coal that left a heavy sooty deposit in the flumes. The boat stopped at Blisworth to draw the fire down, they then remade the fire to build a good head of steam. To help do this they put the blower on, this had the affect of creating a cloud of soot and muck that went skyward, drifted over Blisworth and deposited itself on the unsuspecting inhabitants. The boat, now with a full head of steam, set off into the tunnel. At about one thousand yards in, where today the old tunnel meets the refurbished part, there was some maintenance going on. Apparently this was a spot that was always having to be repaired on a regular basis. There is a geological fault in the tunnel at this point where two plates, one of ironstone and one of clay meet. The result of this is water runs down under the joint and leaks. At the time of the accident they had part of the tunnel sectioned off, there was a channel with just enough room for one boat to pass. Men were working below water level trying to repair the fault, not a pleasant job. As the boat reached this point it slowed down. They were hailed by young William Webb an eighteen year old carpenter from Stoke Bruerne. He had been working in the tunnel and wanted a lift home. He climbed on board the steamer and went under the tarpaulin to keep out of the way as the boat set off again. Soon after this they met two boats coming the other way being legged through in the traditional method of the time. The steamer got past the narrow section and as it drew up alongside the first of the two other boats

the men on that boat said something to Broadbent, he muttered
something in return but they couldn't make out what it was. The
next minute the butty boat that was being towed by the steamer
came down on the other side of the tunnel. Consequently all the
boats became entangled. The smoke from the steamer was dense
so visibility soon became very poor. The men legging the boat
going north crouched down and were very lucky not to sustain
serious injury as the towline whipped over them. By now the fumes
were taking its toll on some of the men, and it was only by a small
miracle that they eventually managed to untangle the ropes. The
towline that had been fastened to the butty boat had been loosed
off, by whom we will never know. The steamer then drifted off on
its own leaving its butty boat behind in the tunnel. The legged boats
managed to get away safely, thinking the chaps on the steamer
would be able to work their way out as well. Unfortunately the two
engineers down in the stoke hole of the steamer were by now being
overcome by the fumes, they fell against the boiler and were
gradually being roasted while unconscious. The steamer came
crawling out of the tunnel at the Stoke Bruerne end with nobody
steering it. Broadbent had been seen at the tiller by another steamer
that was following close behind the legged boats moments earlier,
so what had happened to him? The steamer, out of control, rammed
into the bank. This sudden jolt revived one of the remaining
crewmen who promptly fell overboard. The sudden shock of the
cold water brought him to his senses enough for him to climb back
on board, stop the engine, and close off the steam before passing
out once more. He and the other engineer, were found down in the
boat severely burned. As for William Webb, his body was found
under the tarpaulin where he had died from inhaling the fumes. At
midnight a search boat entered the tunnel to look for Broadbent. On
board was Samuel Harris, one of the leggers from the incident
earlier, he had walked back from Blisworth to help. The tunnel was
dragged from plate fourteen, each plate is one hundred yards,
between plate nine and ten, that's nine hundred to one thousand
yards south of the Blisworth end, the drags caught the body of

Edward Broadbent. What seems to have happened is, after he had been overcome by fumes he fell in to the canal, and was subsequently dragged along by the suction of the passing boat up to the point where the original entanglement occurred. From there his body rested on the bottom under the butty until found by the drag line.

David was reading information from the coroners report of the accident, so we know it is accurate.

Although the tunnel is damp , dark, and claustrophobic, there is still beauty to be seen. Here Richard photographed mineral deposits clinging to the walls, like a waterfall frozen in time.

I then asked David about the information that Judy had received regarding the cave-in. David explained that there had been few fatalities over the years in the tunnel. One persistent legend, to which David can find no documentary evidence, tells of fourteen men dying when the roof caved in. The only evidence David can prove historically, were of two men who died in the air shaft, right where Judy picked up on a feeling of men dying. The shaft is the deepest in the tunnel and is called Blisworth Hill Shaft. The story goes that the two men were being wound up in a bucket, and the rope broke sending them plummeting to their deaths. In fact these, and the boating accident of 1861, are the only documentary evidence of fatalities in the tunnel. David also explained that this is not surprising due to the fact that many coroner reports are incomplete, or missing completely. However, he did say that if fourteen men had died in a cave-in he feels there would have been some reports of it somewhere, it would have been sensational.

Judy also picked up the feeling of a lost child in the year 1912, David thought that was very possible. There had been many reports of lost children from boating families as they go through the tunnel.

David said that because of the fumes and heat on a boat the atmosphere would have been so foul, people very often were forced to lie in the bottom of the boat with a cloth over their faces. Imagine all this, and only being able to see by the light of a tallow candle. It is easy to see how someone could be lost over the side without being noticed.

I told David about the smell of coal fire and steam at a specific point in the tunnel. Luckily we had taken several photos at this point so I hope this would help him pinpoint the place. David looked at the photos and said that they were interesting because they showed heavy sooty deposits on the brickwork. Now this in itself wouldn't mean much to us, but apparently from 1873 until 1936 they had steam tugs to pull the horse drawn boats through. These boats worked to a time schedule and did several pulls a day, so many north, and so many south, working every two hours or so. There was, at that time, very heavy horse drawn traffic and diesel engines didn't appear until the late twenties. The tugs used in the tunnel were very powerful and their boilers had to be at maximum with the safety valves at opening point before the boats started their tunnel run. Once the slack on the towrope had been taken up, the steam in the engine was being used and the safety valves closed.

The aim was to travel through the tunnel without having to fire up the boiler for a second time. However, if the tug was towing several boats there wouldn't be enough steam in the boiler to get them through the tunnel. Firing up the boiler a second time would have to be done at the thousand yard point, half way. The black seen today at that point is the soot left behind from the days of the old tug boats.

During our investigation Judy picked up the name of a company, Hicks & Co, and a fatality related to one of their boats. David said the name sounded familiar and that they may have been one of the many carrier firms operating in the early 1820's to 30's, before the railway took over. Deaths during this time on the canal, even if reported, very rarely made the news. As David said before, records from these times are incomplete. I have worked with Judy before, if she picked up on a fatality in the tunnel chances are it happened.

All the people that made this particular investigation work as well as it did have my thanks. It's not a one man show, all investigations rely on a dedicated team of enthusiasts who spend many hours filming and searching in some very uncomfortable places. Afterwards you search through hours of sound and video footage for that piece of evidence that makes the investigation worthwhile. Blisworth Tunnel has memories of things that happened long ago. It is the memories we picked up on, the energy, not ghosts. If you find yourself approaching the tunnel, from either end, remember this book. See if you can pick up the energy of the people from the past as you drift along in the dark.

The haunted house in Kettering

I received a phone call from a chap who asked me to come to his house if I wanted to see ghosts. From what he told me, and the way it was said, it was clear he wasn't joking. I arranged a date to go over to interview him and his wife. Little did I know at the time just how much this investigation would test, not just me, but many others connected to it. I decided to ask Judy C to accompany me to the house for the initial interview. Judy is very perceptive and I trust her opinion.

The questions you ask on a first interview are of vital importance. The answers enable you to get a feel for the people involved, and help you get a good idea of just what kind of activity you are dealing with.

Alan and Karen live in an end of terrace house close to the centre of Kettering, a town to the east of Northamptonshire. The houses were built in the mid to late nineteenth century to house workers for the boot and shoe industry that was so prevalent at the time. At the time of the interview the couple had been living in the house for about sixteen months. From the very start it was clear the couple were suffering from a great deal of stress and anxiety, now we had to find out why.

Both Alan and Karen are sensitive to spirit and have a history of spirit contact from an early age. Karen comes from Ireland and had something happen to her at the age of five that she will never forget. At that time she was living in England in a block of flats. Her mother would leave biscuits by Karen's bed each evening so she could have a snack. Each night in her bedroom Karen would see hand prints appear on the window. After a while Karen asked her mother not to leave the biscuits in her room because the man comes in and eats them. Her mother thought this was the child's overactive imagination, until she saw the apparition for herself, a dark shadowy figure that seemed menacing. Things escalated quickly after that, Karen's parents had objects thrown at them and also had their bed thrown up into the air. Every time Karen entered a room something would happen. Things came to a head when a priest was called in to calm things down. As soon as the priest entered the flat a plant pot flew across the hall and struck him. He would come no further into the property and said that they would never get rid of the spirit until the child, meaning Karen, was taken away. At the time the case was reported in the local paper, and Karen was called all kinds of unpleasant things, a witch, or the one with the evil eye. Even up to this day, people who know Karen and that story feel uneasy around her. Her parents still think she has the ability to conjure the spirit up at will. Karen is not mad, or evil, or possesses the evil eye, she is a kind, warm hearted woman who is spiritually aware of things around her. Alan has also had paranormal experiences at an early age. As a child in Burton Latimer, Alan saw a large man in his bedroom, his toy cars ran along a corridor in the house on their own, his bed also lifted into the air. The comparison between Alan and Karen's childhood is very close. It seems both are magnets for spirit manifestation. In each house the couple has set up home, spirits follow. The only exception to this being Ireland, where they lived for a short while with no activity whatsoever.

Their house in Kettering is the most haunted house I have ever investigated. It is also, in my opinion, the most haunted house in Northamptonshire. Even while carrying out the initial interview Judy and myself were aware of the presence of spirits in the room with us. There were sudden temperature changes, and sounds from an upstairs room, which we knew to be empty. We were told about things that were being seen by the family on a regular basis. Shadows moving around the living room that Alan had captured on video for us to look at. Furniture moving, voices talking, grotesque ghostly faces at the rear window, and the sound of a dog walking around the house. But probably the most concerning activity was Alan being constantly attacked at night while sleeping in bed. In fact things had reached the point where Alan and Karen were no longer able to sleep upstairs, and were now sleeping in the living room. The attacks were aimed at Alan's legs, constantly being pinched and slapped by an unseen force. He had also been attacked in the bathroom, being cut across the back while shaving. Karen had her hair pulled while watching TV and said she feels threatened while in the house alone. Also living in the house is Alan and Karen's daughter and grandchildren. The granddaughter is three years of age and has seen children playing in her bedroom. On one occasion she came running down the stairs saying the other children won't leave her toys alone, at the time there were no other children in the house. She has also come out with sentences that you would not expect a child of that age to say, they are even too disturbing to put in this book. She has also seen the image of an old woman lying at the bottom of the stairs, with her neck at a strange angle, as if broken. This investigation was one that was desperately needed, and it would need careful thought and preparation if we were to succeed in helping the family.

Alan had tried to contact the spirits within the house to find out what they wanted from him, and why they were there. He had kept a record of events, in video and photo form, if everyone was this organised my job would be a lot easier. Karen was less enthusiastic about the spirits within her home, understandably so. Past experience has taught her to be wary of spirits however friendly they may appear.

As the interview progressed, names and types of spirits that had been experienced came to light. I could hardly believe what I was hearing. To get a sighting, or sound of a spirit, even a poltergeist is a rarity, but to get it all in one house is unheard of. The responsibility of the task ahead was something that struck home quickly. I asked Alan and Karen what result they wanted from the investigation. This may sound silly but it's something you should find out at the start. It's no good clearing spirits from a house if the people are willing to share their home with them. However, this investigation was not going to be that simple. Alan and Karen wanted very different results from us. Alan, who seemed to be the target of the activity, was happy to live with the spirits who were friendly towards him. Karen on the other hand was not going to share her house with any spirit, friendly or not. I have said it before and I am going to say it again, help the family, then sort out spirits. The problem was Alan was losing a great deal of sleep, and for a driver this was bad news. The first vigil would need to be something special, I had an idea of how I wanted to proceed but I would need help. I knew some of the people who had the abilities required for this type of investigation, and I asked others for advice on finding other people with the skills required. I outlined my intentions for the first vigil to Alan and Karen. This would be a double investigation, spiritual, with experienced mediums from the spiritual church to try to clear troublesome spirits and give advice to Alan and Karen, and then the instinctive approach with others from the vigil team. You may be thinking, what is the instinctive approach? Over the years I have learnt to trust my instincts, sixth sense if you like. I know when something is about to kick off and I also pick up on things, spirits and energy. Some of the people working with me have also build up abilities, the longer they do the investigations the better they become at it. The instinctive part of the investigation would deal with identifying how many spirits were present, and how active they were. I knew there would be no quick fix to this one. As the first interview came to an end Judy and myself left Alan and Karen with the promise that I would call them with a date for a vigil.

After a couple of days phoning around a date for the first vigil was set, the 25th of May 2007. Attending, would be Judy, Richard, and myself, with guest mediums James and Natalie. James is an experienced medium who works closely with the spiritual church. Natalie works alongside James and is highly sensitive to spirit, she is also very perceptive.

The vigil on the 25th started hectically. Alan and Karen were both nervous and a little apprehensive, as were other members of the family who were there when we arrived. It took about an hour for things to start to settle down to a point where we could sit and chat without to many interruptions. Staying with Alan and Karen that night was Sarah, one of their grown up daughters. None of the children would be in the house. Children should always be out of a house if you are going to conduct a paranormal investigation. James and Natalie could not stay all night, so the spiritual investigation would be done first. James would lead this, with Judy and Natalie giving advice to the people present. They would have a brief look around the house, then we would all sit in a circle to try to find out what the spirits wanted. People present for the circle would be, Alan, Karen, Sarah, Richard, Judy, Natalie, James, and myself. It was clear from the start of the evening that this was not going to be easy. Sarah was extremely anxious and hyper, not through spirit activity, she was just anxious about the evening ahead. We always give people the opportunity to observe and not take part in a circle. Sarah was determine to stay, so Judy sat with her before and during the circle quietly reassuring her.

James and Natalie had a look around and pinpointed the hotspots within the house. The hallway, top of the stairs, middle and front bedrooms and living room were all active. As we sat down for the circle I asked Alan and Karen to bring James and Natalie up to speed as far as recent activity was concerned. As Alan explained how he was being attacked during the night, and the family's history with spirits, I could see James trying to take it all in. Even for an experienced medium this level of activity is extremely rare. James then asked Alan, if he could wave a magic wand and make things better for him, how would he like things to be within the house. Alan replied that he just wanted the spirits that were attacking him to stop. He wasn't worried about the others, he could live with them. At this point Karen said she didn't want any spirits in the house at all. She explained that she knew spirits could seem friendly, but could change within moments, she had had first hand experience and she wanted them out of her home. Karen was now getting very upset and things needed calming down before we could go any further. Judy teaches meditation and relaxation, so to lead into the spiritual part of the investigation she put on some soothing music and began to help people relax. This isn't just a relaxation class, it is a vital part of allowing yourself to be protected within the circle and to open the mind, allowing spirit to contact us if they wish to. Even if you do not contact spirit, it is a very pleasant way of recharging the batteries. Judy told us what to look out for during the circle, and what to do if an individual was contacted by a spirit. This may sound silly to some, but knowing what to do within a group is important.

It took another thirty minutes to get to a point where people were happy and relaxed, and it was Natalie who began to get the first spirit contact. A young man in motorcycle gear, who Natalie thought was related to Alan, had died in an accident and wanted to make contact with him. Alan said he did have a cousin who died in a motorcycle accident, but the cousin was female. Natalie was convinced this was a male spirit contacting her and the name Ray was given. Karen then realised that Natalie's spirit contact was for her. When younger she had hung around with bikers and been in an accident on a motorcycle with a chap called Ray, but he hadn't died. Natalie then saw in her mind the picture of a rose and a dagger, possibly tattoos. Alan said he had tattoos on his arms, on one side a rose, and on the other a dagger. Natalie could not have known this as Alan was wearing long sleeves. Information during a circle can, and very often is, unstructured. With eight people sitting in a circle it is hard for a medium to know just what information relates to which individual. Natalie also managed to pick up on information related to an investigation I was working on, it actually helped me decide which way to proceed.

During the circle I managed to picked up on a woman who lived next door during the first world war who had lost her husband. It seems she visits Alan in times of stress, in a comforting and caring way she tries to help him. Alan said he has felt the presence of a female spirit on various occasions, now he knows who it is.

The circle was successful, as much as we did pick up on spirit and identified them, but Alan and Karen wanted to know who the spirits were that were violent towards them, this we had not achieved. We could all sense their frustration as the circle ended. With this in mind James decided to try, with the help of Natalie and Judy, to help the spirits that were trapped within the property move on to a higher level within the spirit world. Alan and Karen asked them to try to clear the bedrooms, hopefully to give them a good nights sleep. While this was in progress Richard and myself prepared for the instinctive investigation, deciding what to do, where and when to do it. Sometimes this works well and other times you simply go with what happens. James, Natalie and Judy were pleased with the clearance done in the bedrooms. They stayed on for a while and chatted with Alan and Karen about the other spirits within the house that come and go on a regular basis.

Alan and Karen sent out for some pizza so we could all have a break at around midnight. Judy decided to stay as long as she could into the early hours to help in the other investigation. James and Natalie had to leave as close to midnight as possible, after pizza though. While we were all eating and chatting Alan showed us some of the photos he had taken in the house of the spirits that were regular visitors. I have to say I wasn't too surprised having spoken to Alan about them, but the look on the faces of the others spoke volumes, they suddenly realised what they were up against. This was not the odd photo, Alan had video tape and EVP (Electronic Voice Phenomena) recordings.

Shortly after James and Natalie left we started the second part of the investigation. To describe how it works is difficult, but I will do my best. When you have a property with only a small amount of spirit activity and you have a small investigation group, it is easier than a property with loads of activity and a large investigation group. Spirits are not stupid, go in mob handed and you will achieve nothing. If you go in with sensitivity and a real willingness to help, you will achieve your goal. I always encourage the owners of the property to actively take part in an investigation. Alan and Karen needed no encouragement, they were ready to take part and help in any way they could. This confirmed for me that what was happening in their home was not faked, they were always open with any information we needed.

I asked Richard to conduct a vigil in the centre bedroom for an hour or so, he always seems to be able to photograph activity where ever he is. I also asked him to do any experiments that he thought may get results. Sarah joined Richard, and the two of them set up cameras and sound equipment. The experiment they decided to do was to place a light in the front bedroom along with a digital sound recorder, the door to that bedroom was then closed. They opened the door to the back bedroom and returned to the middle bedroom, turned the lights off and trained the cameras on the landing area, waiting for something to happen. Meanwhile I sat with Judy, Alan, and Karen in the living room quietly chatting while waiting for some activity to occur. Only moments into the vigil we all heard the sound of a dog walking along the hallway, its claws tapping on the laminated flooring as it walked. Richard and Sarah confirmed they could also hear it. The door to the hallway from the living room was closed and had glass panels from top to bottom, we could hear the footsteps but see nothing. I think it was Judy who said, pity it doesn't come in here, instantly the closed living room door swung open and a strong gust of icy cold air blasted over us. We instantly took some photographs and the results were amazing.

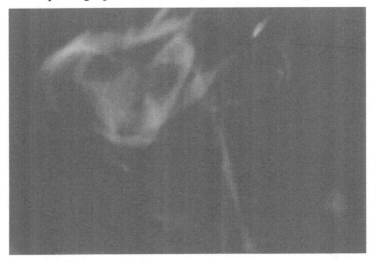

Alan took this shot with his digital camera, although nothing could be seen at the time. Alan had been thinking about the pet dog he once had while we were listening to the footsteps in the hallway.

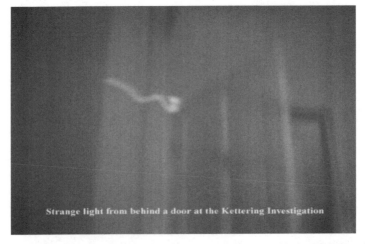

Strange light from behind a door at the Kettering Investigation

This activity heralded activity upstairs as well. As Richard and Sarah watched the landing, a light from the front bedroom lit up the wall. Someone, or something, had opened the front bedroom door illuminating the landing. Richard then took a shot of the door on the landing, a strange light was seen moving from the top corner after the door had opened.

Things then settled down for a while. In fact this became a notable pattern, surges of activity followed by calmer periods of inactivity. The way our vigils seem to work, is with people not trying to contact the spirits directly, but by introducing them into simple conversations. Richard and Sarah came downstairs and joined in our little chill out session in the living room. Judy unfortunately had to go home due to commitments later that day. This was unfortunate as we knew she was enjoying the experience. As it happened this loss of another person seemed to confirm what I had thought about sizes of groups on investigations, activity started up again. We heard walking in the bedrooms above our heads, captured sounds on recorders, and saw shapes moving in the kitchen.

The investigation team at work in Kettering.

All too soon our time was up and daylight came through the cracks in the closed curtains. I knew this investigation was going to be no quick fix, and I discussed this with Alan and Karen. Although we had proof of activity within the property, this was not what we were there for. We were there to help the family rid themselves of the violent spirits, and if possible, live with the spirits that reside within the house. We needed to identify who the spirits were, some of this we had done, and also why the spirits were haunting them, yet to do. A date was fixed for our return and we said our goodbyes.

On the 29th of June we were back at the house to do vigil 2. I wanted to cover more rooms in the house simultaneously, obviously this would need about the same number of people as before, something I really wanted to avoid. Attending this vigil were, Alan, Karen, and their two adult sons. From the vigil team were Lisa, Richard, and myself, with guest Emma Whiteman, founder of the newly formed Northampton Paranormal group.

I wanted to throw everything at it this time. I also wanted people to be open and truthful about what they thought and how they were feeling. Richard had already walked around the house when we first arrived and reported strange feelings upstairs in the front and middle bedrooms. I decided on a circle to settle us all down, and then split up and spread out to see what would happen. During the circle footsteps were heard above our head in the front bedroom. Lights were seen in one corner of the room where we were sitting. Unfortunately no photos of the lights could be taken due to a power drain in a camera that had only just been charged minutes before. Lisa had reported having severe back pain while sitting in the circle. This could be due to the fact she is developing healing powers, and she was sitting between two people with chronic back pain, the pain disappeared when the circle broke up. Something else to note is the digital recorder set to run during the circle, had switched itself off. We stopped the investigation for a while to have something to eat and drink. As we chatted more noises were heard upstairs. Deciding to investigate I climbed the stairs to the landing and was convinced I saw someone in the middle bedroom. Thinking it was one of the group, I said, "I thought someone was up here" then went down again, only to see everyone was there. The hair stood up on the back of my neck and a cold shiver shot down my spine. During the break Alan showed the group video footage of a dark shadow moving about the living room. Everything in the living room was being recorded at a normal speed, but the shadow was moving at incredibly high speed, even slowed down you could only see a blurred dark shadow. It was the same height of a person, but nobody could move that fast.

After the break the vigil continued with three people upstairs, one in the kitchen, one in the bathroom and three in the living room. The reason there was one person in the bathroom was, Alan had recorded two unseen people talking in there. Would they return? We hoped so. While chatting on the settee the sound of something rolling across the fireplace was heard by myself and Emma. After a while we decided to swap locations. Karen heard someone breathing by her shoulder as she left the kitchen, this had happened to her before in that location.

Up to now nothing had happened to the people upstairs, even the sounds we were hearing up there from down in the living room were not being heard up there. People were capturing orbs where activity was being seen or heard.

What happened next was a surprise, I don't know why, we should have been expecting it, but it took us all by surprise. Alan was sitting close by the french windows in the living room when he heard a voice whisper close to his ear. Our attention was seized as he asked whoever it was to repeat what they had said because he had not understood it. Alan's sons were sitting close to him and they also thought they could hear the voice. The voice was so faint the voice operated Dictaphone could not register it. It then repeated, "Alan I am here". The voice was male and sounded insistent, it was also heard by three people in the room. This was followed shortly afterward by the sound of soft breathing. Alan was touched on the leg, and Richard felt a cold blast to his legs, he could also hear whistling coming from the kitchen. He asked me to swap places so I could hear it. I began to hear knocking from the kitchen door which was heard by four other people in the group. Then Emma, Richard, and myself heard a noise directly behind me as if something was being put down on a work surface. After a while things settled down again and all was quiet. By this time everyone was in the living room listening and watching for the slightest movement. I decided to do a solo vigil in the front bedroom, without success. There was a flurry of activity from outside when one of Alan and Karen's sons was poked in the eye while filming out there. I asked Alan and Karen to go upstairs and lay on the bed as normal to see if the attacks started up while we were there. Even this did not stir the spirits into activity. The fact was we were all now suffering from tiredness and complacency, the kiss of death to an investigation. We all agreed to stop and call it a night. I asked Alan and Karen later how they felt the vigil had gone. They thought there was too much camera flashing and a smaller group would work better. I agreed with this and said I would be in touch to chat about a further vigil.

Now this may sound strange to anyone new to paranormal investigating, but all the people attending this vigil were, on reflection, disappointed with the evenings events. The problem was people went with high expectations and we suffered from long bouts of inactivity leading to complacency and fatigue. Alan and Karen were of the same opinion as myself when it comes to numbers attending vigils, keep it small. A date for vigil three was set for October the 12th 2007 and a 10.00pm start. Only Richard and myself would be with Alan and Karen for this one, and hopefully we would have better luck.

Our preparation for vigil three was meticulous, clean tapes, new and fully recharged batteries, empty memory cards on equipment, and everything tested beforehand. What could go wrong? Yeah right, I should have known better. Five minutes into the investigation and I lost all power to the infrared lighting and digital recorder. Karen used a laser thermometer and noted a marked temperature drop around the equipment that had failed, the rest of the room was normal temperature. Richard took several shots in the direction of the cold spot but these showed nothing unusual. Alan then showed us photos he had taken the evening before of hand prints that had appeared on the outside of the french windows.

Strange hand prints on a back door at the Kettering investigation.
Much larger than ours. Five minutes later they had vanished
leaving no trace.

Karen and Alan said the hand prints did not fit anyone in the house and there is no access to the rear garden, five minutes later they had gone. It is interesting now to remember that when Karen was a young girl she saw hand prints on her bedroom window. Pictures taken of the living room mirror show white lines around the room in the reflection. Alan then said that preparing for work one morning that week he had heard a voice ask, "Where is Beverley". A conversation with a neighbour shed some light on this. Apparently, two people had died of cancer in the house, the bed was situated in the living room and one of the people was called Beverley. Alan explained that he thought the main spirit in the house is that of a young girl, she is always asking for his help, and he thinks she is the one constantly doing things, I believe this to be true. I have picked up on a young girl on two occasions within the living room and kitchen. She is about sixteen years of age and of small build, she also seems to like wearing a baseball cap on backwards, her name is Sarah. There was a Sarah that went missing some years ago from around here and she was never found. Karen said she feels uncomfortable in the bathroom and sometimes in the

55

kitchen when she is on her own in the house. The bathroom is only a few years old and is an extension on the kitchen. Alan has recorded voices on a digital recorder in the bathroom, and their daughter Sarah has had the door jammed on her on several occasions. Other children in the house said they have seen a man standing in the bathroom, staring at them. The children have also heard a man in the bedroom saying," Alan dead". It's worth noting at this point that Karen seems more relaxed when talking about the spirits in her home that when we first met. Alan's viewpoint has not changed, he is intrigued and wants to find out who they are and what they want.

About an hour into the investigation Alan, Karen, and myself sat talking about things in the living room with all the lights off when suddenly the infrared camera sprang into life. Richard was doing a solo vigil in the front bedroom and was getting knocking and banging. He tried to record the sounds but they were too faint. Downstairs we were quite relaxed. Alan went to the bathroom, and as he returned there was a brilliant flash of light in the kitchen behind him as he walked through. He was quite unaware it had happened, but I caught it on video so I know it wasn't my imagination. Another temperature drop heralded a spate of activity in the kitchen with shadows and strange lights being seen. Movement close to us in the living room was also heard moments after that. Now during all this we had digital sound recorders going, and when played back we heard a dog barking, and at a point when Alan said, "Is there a Mary in here", a voice is clearly heard saying, "No my name is Peter".

By now we all needed a break, so Alan said he would make a cup of tea, on went the lights and Richard came down stairs. The next photo you can see was taken by Richard during the break. Looks like the ghosts behind Alan wanted a drink.

The research I had done into the history of the house had shown pastureland up until the 1850's. As I said earlier houses were then built for the boot and shoe industry. I had searched back to 1587, when Kettering was nothing but a small collection of dwellings with a church. The problem you hit while doing such research is when you reach the cut off point. Celtic, Roman, and medieval history is not recorded. Only archeological records can go back further, and to my knowledge no records exists for this part of Kettering. There could have been a burial ground here, crossroads, or even a medieval village, we simply do not know. From the evidence so far it seems that the spirits within the house are fairly modern, I say modern, I mean from the mid 1800's onward, only the black shadowy figure was causing me concern. I needed to find out more from Alan and Karen regarding the everyday activity of the spirits. What time of the day, week, month, or year does the activity increase. They both agreed that Christmas was a time for increased activity, especially around the children. As this is a time of family gatherings, when energy levels are at their highest, maybe the spirits are attracted by the emotions generated within this family. But Alan said the actual activity is happening every day, without fail.

Up to now the only spirit to ask Alan for help is called Sarah. The one Alan thought was called Mary, we now know is actually a male called Peter, what he wants we have yet to find out. There are also spirits outside in the back garden that we know for some reason can't enter the house. This is something else we have to find the answer to. Karen described one of the spirits she has seen in the garden, he was leaning on the rubbish bin, wearing a cap, white shirt with sleeves rolled up, open waistcoat, black trousers with braces, and black work boots. This clothing is typical of the boot and shoe period. Alan has also taken photos of spirits looking at his young grandchildren.

As we sat in the dark waiting for more to happen, we could all hear whispering voices. I remember thinking, this is not going to be easy to stop, Alan and Karen are drawing the spirits to them wherever they live. I was in a situation that I knew I could only partially help them. I could find out who and why, but as for stopping it, I had my doubts. It was agreed that we would do

57

From the Kettering investigation.
Look at the man in the centre of the shot.
What is standing behind him?

another vigil early in the new year. I certainly needed time to sit and go through all the videos and start writing the story. Where would it end? As yet I couldn't say.

On the 8th of February 2008 we were back at the house to try to conclude the investigation with Richard, Ken, and myself. By now Richard was well aware of what was possible in the house and Alan and Karen are comfortable with him in their home. Ken is a good photographer who, as you are now aware, has worked with me on several investigations, he stays calm when things get active so he was going to be helpful doing solo investigations in various parts of the house. There were three main things I needed to know from this vigil, One, why and how did Sarah want Alan to help her? Two, who was Peter? Three, why couldn't the spirits in the garden enter the house?

When we arrived it was nice to see everyone was relaxed and calm, this was going to be a good vigil, you could feel it. After settling in and catching up with Alan and Karen I asked Richard and Ken to go around the house to do some tests, EMF, RF, and temperature readings. During the course of the night we would monitor the same spots to see how things change, if they change. Even while Ken and Richard were doing their tests they felt they were being watched, the feelings were so strong they looked round to see if anyone was there. On our last visit to the house interesting

EVP's had been recorded, so this time we had an abundance of digital recorders with us and left them in various locations around the house. Ken and Richard were itching to start the vigil so they set off upstairs to cover the front and rear bedrooms and place movement sensors on the landing, I remained downstairs with Alan and Karen in the living room. When everyone was in place we switched off all the lights and settled down to see what would happen. The first thing I heard was a little girls voice close to where we were sitting. The words were unrecognisable and muffled but definitely that of a young girl. I started to ask who was present with us in the room, Alan then heard a female voice in answer to the name Sarah. It is a strange fact that during investigations at this house, although being in one of the busiest parts of Kettering the silence within the property is almost total, only broken by our spirit friends. I think this is why we can hear the voices and whispers so clearly. Karen describes the silence as deathly, that is a very accurate description indeed. Ten minutes after the lights had gone out we heard shuffling movements in the kitchen, and at the same time an orb was seen floating across the video camera. Minutes later a light flashed in the corner behind Karen, sadly not captured on film. Alan explained that the corner where the light had appeared was a very active part of the room, and when he sits there he can usually hear whispering. The corner is just to the right of the french windows where several spirits have been photographed in the past. We know from asking local people that a few years ago two residents slept in this room before finally succumbing to cancer. After a while it became noticeably cold in the area I was sitting, interestingly Karen also felt cold, but Alan who was sitting next to her felt quite warm. When a building is cooling down during the night it is usually a gradual overall affect. When you get distinct cold spots, and I mean cold, it means something is about to happen. Sure enough there was a growling noise that came from behind the settee where Karen sat. She was a little concerned at this point and this wasn't helped when movement was also heard from the same spot. Alan told her not to worry as he had heard the noises before. Things then settled down for a while and we started to chat about this and that. During our conversations it came to light that the street where the house is built, and the next street, are built on, guess what, a plague pit. With this, and the fact that Alan and Karen are hyper sensitive, no wonder the spirits are in, and around the house, it all made perfect sense now. If you are born with a high ability to sense spirits you can't just turn it off, it's with you for life. That is why wherever these two live they encounter spirit, and they hit the jackpot here. Karen then said that when they go to live in Ireland they are never bothered by spirits. She believes that spirits can't travel over water. I have never heard this theory before. It could be that because she believes this, it somehow blocks out the thought process that allows spirit in. Now that is something science should investigate.

Things started to happen around us again with shadows moving behind and in front of us. Alan saw a shadowy figure drift across behind my video camera, interestingly when played back, just before he mentions it the camera flickers. Shadows were also seen moving in the kitchen, and in the hallway through the glass door. It was now an hour into the investigation and we heard Ken and Richard walking about and talking upstairs, something had obviously happened. Alan and Karen switched the lights on made some tea while we waited for the lads to come down. While we all sat drinking tea Ken told us he had experienced knocks and tapping in the front bedroom. These sounds had moved down the bed and across the room, at the same time the curtains had started to move in and out, as if breathing. As soon as Ken reached for his camcorder the movement stopped, he also checked for drafts and found nothing. He decided to experiment with the laser thermometer and checked the walls within the room. The outside wall was, as expected, slightly colder than the inner walls, however, when he measured the window temperature it was the hottest part of the room at a constant 18.3. Knowing this wasn't as it should be Ken decided to do another experiment. He pointed the laser at the window, which still read 18.3, and asked "If you are here can you make the temperature go down", instantly the temperature dropped down to 17.4. At this point Richard entered the room and the experiment stopped. Ken then had a name come into his head, Billy, the name wasn't recognised, but that doesn't mean it won't be later on. Richard reported no activity at all in the back bedroom and no temperature fluctuations. A while later as we sat chatting Karen explained to Ken about activity that had been experienced during the daytime in the middle bedroom some weeks before. Apparently while a friend was visiting her there were loud banging and knocking sounds emanating from that bedroom, as if someone was slamming doors and stamping on the floor. Bravely her friend went up to investigate and found all the cupboard doors and drawers open. The children in the house have all experienced paranormal events at some level. I must just stress at this point than no children were present during any of the vigils we performed in the house. Karen also explained that we, as investigators, only see what happens during one night, imagine having this happening every day, you now have some idea of what this family is going through.

Richard and Ken at Kettering

After taking some photos around the living room we settled into the investigation again, this time I would tackle the front bedroom while Ken and Richard experienced the living room. Upstairs I opened all the bedroom doors and then settled myself down on the bed in the front bedroom. As my eyes became accustomed to the light I could see into the rear bedroom to the far end of the hall and landing. There were motion sensors half way across the hallway so anything physical passing them would set them off. I started asking for the spirits that we knew were in the house to come to me and make their presence felt. Straight away there was shuffling in the back bedroom, and what looked like amber eyes blinking close to the floor. I quickly took a photo of these and to my astonishment they appeared on the screen.

As soon as I took the shot the eyes disappeared, cautiously I investigated the room but found nothing. I settled back down on the bed and tried to capture some EVP's. This is a simple process, you switch on your recorder and ask a specific question, pause for a few seconds and then play the recording back. Astonishingly I recorded the sound of a dog barking after asking for Peter to contact me. I heard nothing while asking out, but the recorder captured the sound. Here is a tip for the would-be investigator, do not do endless hours of recording, instead do several smaller recordings. By doing this you are able to pinpoint any activity, finding it quicker. You can also isolate the shorter recording and sample it on the computer at a later date. Things for me went very quiet after this initial activity. I could see flash photography being done downstairs so I knew they were having better luck, I decided to sit it out and wait to see if things started up again. Meanwhile downstairs in the living room Alan was asking for specific spirits to make contact with them. There was activity in answer to the name Sarah. Ken then asked her to send the temperature down, it started at 16.0 and fell dramatically down to 14.0. There was also a sudden bright red flash of light in the corner by the french windows, recorded on video. Richard was touched on the leg and the temperature plummeted down to around 13.0, then as they watched it fell to 12.4. Ken then saw the shape of someone standing in front of the french windows, it lasted only seconds and as it disappeared the temperature rose to 16.4. Richard and Karen saw a shadow by the cooker in the kitchen. I decided to join them downstairs as I had experienced no more activity. The time was 12.50 am.

Frustratingly as I came down to the living room we heard walking in the front bedroom. Richard said he would investigate and disappeared upstairs. We stopped again for a break and to change films in the video cameras. As we did this Alan's two digital recorders both switched off simultaneously. These were eighty eight hour recorders so we knew they were not full, and the batteries were still good. As Richard came down from upstairs I distinctly heard a dog bark in the hallway, Richard then entered the room and asked if we had heard the sound. He had heard it while half way down the stairs. Alan then captured a surname on EVP, it sent a shiver down our spines as we heard a spirit voice say Alan's surname. We switched off the lights and settled in for another stint. There seemed to be a distinct lack of activity for about an hour or so, then came some knocking from upstairs. It was Ken who now decided to check out the sounds, so he decided to do a solo vigil in the front bedroom. Alan told him to lay down on the bed, that's when things tend to kick off.

After a while I started asking out for Sarah to speak to us, Alan then played back the digital recording he had made while I was asking her to speak. His recording had a voice saying, "Come and get me". Ken experienced very little activity while upstairs, some knocking and slight tapping noises, but apart from that nothing.

We gave it another hour but were all getting quite tired by now. Deciding to call it a night we packed away our equipment. The investigation was a success on all counts. Alan was not being attacked any more, Karen was now more interested in spirits than scared of them, and we had all become good friends over the last twelve months. We know why the spirits are there, and who most of them are. However, Alan and Karen have decided to move house, through necessity rather than being forced out by the ghosts. In fact they are only moving about two streets away . They said if they get ghosts in that house, (more than likely) then we will be back on the trail once again. We thanked them for their warm hospitality and made our way home.

Remember this. If you are born with a sensitivity to see or hear spirits , then you will do so for the rest of your life, no matter where you live. I wish Alan, Karen, and the whole family a happy and interesting future.

The Haunted Shop In Bedford

A friend of mine rang one evening inviting me to an investigation at a shop in Bedford. He said the shop was in the process of being refurbished and there had been reports of paranormal activity experienced by several people over the last few weeks. Apparently another investigation group had spent time in the shop and had concluded that there was indeed activity in several areas. At the start of this investigation I knew nothing of the history surrounding the shop, or of the people that were closely attached to it . As you may have already guessed by now this is how I like to start an investigation. The friend who had invited me on the investigation was Andy Ellis, he has known the family who own the shop for over twenty years so could verify any information people picked up on during the course of the investigation. You may recognise Andy's name, he is a regular member of the vigil team and has worked with me on several investigations in the past.

Let me try to describe the layout of the shop for you. This is not going to be easy so bear with me a little. Leading in off the street the ground floor of the shop covers a large area. In fact above the shop are two terrace houses with living areas and bedrooms above that. These dwellings are now incorporated with the shop and are used as storage areas. What were once gardens to the rear have now become an extension to the main shop. The only partition on the ground floor is the supporting wall to the two houses above. There is also a small cellar to one side of the shop. I told you it wasn't going to be easy. Most of the night vision photos you will see are taken from infrared video footage. The camera was positioned on the ground floor at the back of the shop pointing towards the front and the main street beyond. I will explain where other photos were taken as we go through the investigation. With me for the first investigation were, Richard, Judy, Lisa, Mark, and Andy. Others involved with the investigation were Kevin and Julie from the paranormal group who had been in there before, and Peter, from the family who own the shop. Right! We know nothing as yet, so how do we proceed. A circle downstairs and a vigil upstairs was a good starting point, it would give all those present time to calm down and focus on the job in hand. Andy, Mark, Lisa and Richard were to start the vigil upstairs, and the rest of us would start a circle downstairs. Questions to answer, do we have spirits or ghosts, or both? Kevin and Julie, from APIS were keeping quiet, but were keen to see how we would get on during the night. I asked Judy to start the circle, and we were off and running. During a circle it takes time to build up the energy within the group, you all need to be focused. It's a bit like tuning into a radio station, the trick is in getting everyone in the circle onto the same waveband. You soon know when it's working well, you can almost feel what someone is about to say before they even speak. When this happens you can contact any spirits close to you who are willing to join with you, and join us they did. Judy was the first to pick up on someone, it was a young boy who visited the property when the houses were being lived in, she also got a mental picture of a delivery bike, you know, the type with a basket on the front. The young lad used to come in the back way on the delivery bike, and Judy said she thought it had something to do with bread, fish or meat. Now Kevin also started to pick up on the same image, and boy, working together more information started to emerge. A date of 1910 was picked out and the boy wore a white apron and flat cap while doing his delivery. The firm was called Wrights and Son and the delivery boys name was Billy. There were no feelings of malice within the building, just a warm feeling of welcome. Other people that were picked up on during the first circle were, an old man with a walking stick, bent over with a stoop, possibly with the name of Ivan. A large woman with what seemed to be large jars of sweets. I picked up on a woman who I believed lived over the shops in 1876, and whose husband died here, her name was Isabel Chambers, Bella for short. She was dressed in a long dress with puffed shoulders and had a bun hairstyle. All these people lived or worked here in the past and the circle was working particularly well, we hoped the vigil upstairs was working as well. The vigil team from upstairs came down just as we finished our circle, I say just finished, Judy

67

was finding it hard to stop thinking about a woman she had had contact with earlier. The vigil team had photographed orbs in the rooms upstairs and had heard some knocking and banging, the source of which could not be found.

(Below) Even when the vigil team came downstairs orbs seem to take an interest in them, this one was close to the floor behind Richard and Mark.

Filming at the Bedford shop

It was decided to join forces in a large circle to try to get to the bottom of who the spirits were. The only person not in the circle was Richard who had decided to go solo in the upper rooms. Sometimes this works as the spirits seem to like to contact people on their own. It takes nerve, but Richard enjoys the challenge.

Immediately after the circle started, we were getting results. It was Kevin who began to pick up on several children who were suffering from sickness. Interestingly, it seemed that a child related to one of the child spirits, and living now, was also suffering from sickness, there was a link developing. A woman spirit wanted us to know they were aware of the sick child and that things would be alright. Richard suddenly appeared saying he had lost power from his batteries almost immediately after calling out upstairs, but they were new ones. Andy, who you remember was upstairs during the first circle, started to pick up on Isabel, even to the point of describing her. The detail of information between the two groups was astonishing. But there is a possibility the two groups could have overheard each other. More names and dates came thick and fast, all of which would need verifying later.

For the next part of the investigation it was decided to split up into smaller groups, to cover the largest amount of rooms possible. Mark and Richard decided to investigate the cellar, Kevin, Julie, Judy, Lisa and Peter, were upstairs in the rooms to the left, and Andy and myself were in the rooms upstairs to the right. After a while Richard and Mark gave up in the cellar with no activity to report and decided to explore the ground floor. Again the sound of voices from the other two groups could be heard clearly, not helping the two on the ground floor, effectively ruling out their investigation. It has to be said when this happens it is really frustrating, but this frequently happens in empty buildings. It was Kevin who had the most dramatic event of the evening. Whilst investigating the rooms to the left he experienced a psychic attack, so strong he had to leave the building for several minutes. If you are wondering what a psychic attack is, it's when you become overwhelmed by a spirit, whether intentional or not. Sometime

69

spirits get carried away with the chance to speak through someone, or a spirit can get annoyed with you for not allowing them to join with you. Whatever the reason, when it happens it is extremely unpleasant. When Kevin returned he said that he had encountered an angry spirit. They had already received knocking sounds in answer to questions asked, and Kevin had felt the energy within the room building, the trouble was it built too much. Even after Kevin had left the room Judy and the others were still hearing sounds and knocking in answer to simple questions. As for Andy and myself, things were quieter. We did have the feeling we were being watched and followed around by an unseen presence, but nothing more than that. It was when we went downstairs and joined Kevin, Richard, and Mark, that things really became interesting. Andy, who is becoming a good natural medium, began to pick up on a very strong male spirit. I managed to film the whole event, and it has to be said it is one of the most impressive pieces of mediumship I have seen for years.

Andy picking up on the spirit of the shop owner. Take note of where he is standing.

This orb was shot minutes after Andy had connected with the owner. In exactly the same spot.

It started with an icy blast that blew across Andy's face. This heralded a visit from a strong male spirit dressed in a white T-shirt, blue V-neck sweater, and dark trousers . The spirit told Andy that this was his space. Kevin asked Andy to get the spirit to explain what he meant by his space. The spirit said that he sits just inside the shop and watches people come and go, he enjoys seeing them. The spirit gave his name as Richard, and said he was the previous owner, this was Peter's father. Unfortunately Peter had just left us as he needed to be up early in the morning. Andy then went on to describe Richard to us. He wore glasses, had dark hair and was of stocky build. Kevin said he had picked Richard up before and that he usually wore a sheepskin coat. Andy said Richard was sad to see the shop in the state it was. Sadly the shop has closed after many years of being a gents outfitters, through no fault of anyone it is simply a sign of the times. Peoples tastes have changed over the years and even trying to sell the latest fashions didn't help. Andy explained that Richard was a shopkeeper of the old school. When alive he was always in the shop and chatted with the customers when they came in to buy something, people even came in to chat with him when they didn't want anything. The shop, and Richard, were part of the community, sadly community spirit seems to be a distant memory in many towns these days, profit above all else. Richard's spirit was saddened by events and just wanted to let the family know he was around. Spirits are not stupid, they know why we do what we do. Even if they do not agree with the decisions we make, they know why we make them. The shops are going to be renovated and used as shops again so I think Richard will be content. Andy was linked into Richard so strongly that the strength of contact became too much for him, Andy was forced to break away and end the link. I for one thought the contact was real and spontaneous, this is when the best flow of information is available to us from the spirit world. Remember this, spirits only contact the living when they have a good reason to, and no other time.

Night vision shot of the group at Bedford

The rest of the vigil was rather quiet, so after the circle concluded, it was decided to call it a night. We had recognised one main spirit and identified several others. Looking back at the night vision video later there were orbs around us while the first circle was being done, and orbs around Andy while he was in contact with the spirit of Richard. I would look forward to vigil two with anticipation. In the meantime I was up to my neck in writing, setting up more investigations, and answering peoples questions on the internet. The people I work with, with the odd exception, have full time jobs. They investigate the paranormal in their spare time. None of us have large sums of money to throw at the investigations, everything is done on a tight budget. But if you were to see the dedication and professionalism in the way they conduct investigations you would be surprised. It's not the funded scientific community who will find the answers to paranormal questions, it's the kind of people who work with me that will find the answers. It's not a job, it's a passion.

I was itching to get back to Bedford and to find out more about the shop, and I didn't have long to wait. Andy contacted me within weeks and we were off again. Attending vigil two were, Andy, Judy, Richard and his friend, Lisa and her brother Ashley, and myself. We didn't hang around on this investigation. We knew the layout, and the hotspots, so we were ready to do the investigation as soon as we arrived. We split into two groups, one of three, Judy, Andy ,and myself, and one of four, Lisa, Ashley, Richard and his friend. The four of them went up to the rooms on the left, and our group of three decided to try to pick up on the spirits on the ground floor where Andy had picked up on the spirit Richard the previous owner. It was good to have Judy with us, knowing how strong some of the spirits are, she would be able to calm things down should they become too energised. We didn't have to wait long before Andy picked up on a rather defensive male spirit. This time it was Judy who was working with Andy, providing a caring reassuring voice that definitely helped in the situation we found ourselves. There were knocks and banging around us that increased in frequency as the spirit seemed to get annoyed at our questioning. I could sense something but decided not to become involved at the start, sometimes it's better to see how things progress before

73

making the decision to get involved. The spirit reluctantly identified himself as a man who had experienced fire, whether at the shop or not we could not say, but at one point all three of us could smell burning. The spirit seemed to blame himself for not returning to, or for starting a fire. He also worked with fire, and had an Italian accent and said his name was Jack Gilespie Interestingly at this point on the video Judy's voice took on a deep male tone that none of us were aware of at the time. I then realised that I was picking up on a man working at a smelting works, obviously a steelworker, could it be Jack? I was then given the name Britannia, and Andy recognised this as the Britannia Steel Works that date back to around the 1850's. As fast as the spirit had come to us he had gone, that was really frustrating as we knew we were getting somewhere. It was time for a break and to see how the other group had got on. Again they reported knocking in answer to questions asked. Lisa also reported being touched on two occasions. She said it was like a prickly sensation, and happened while we were all having a break and drinking tea, but it definitely happened.

After a break we were off again. Ashley and myself went down into the cellar to do a vigil, while the rest of the group went back upstairs to try in the rooms again. There seems to be a cut off point for activity in the shop, at 2.00 am all goes quiet. It happened last time, and it was happening again. In the cellar we experienced nothing, and upstairs all that was experienced was a feeling of being followed around from room to room. Time to call it a day. Yet again we had recorded more information and that's what it's all about. I would be back with another team a few weeks later, and boy were we in for a surprise.

Attending vigil 3 were, Andy, Mark, Paul, Gill, Matt, Lewis and myself. Andy and Mark you have met before, Paul has worked with us at Twinwood farm in the past, Gill and Matt are interested in the paranormal, Matt is not a believer as yet, but that's not a bad thing on an investigation. Lewis is training in Parapsychology and is a good level headed chap to have around. You will find an interview I did with Lewis later on in the book.

This vigil started more as a social event and drifted gently into the investigation. It's nice to be able to do this, especially if you had not seen each other for a while. So after a fish and chip supper and a drink we were all relaxed and in good spirits, so to speak. Gill and Matt had started exploring the property first before the rest of us began. This was a good decision on their part as it gave them time to get a feel for the place without having us around. We sometimes forget that a new investigator on any investigation may need time to get up to speed on past events and the current feel of a property. The feeling of being left out can make a vigil feel a complete waste of time to them. This is something to remember if you are planning a vigil in a location you already know.

During some frank discussions on paranormal techniques and methods between Lewis, Gill and Matt, Andy and Paul were doing some wandering between the upper rooms of the property. When they joined us back down in the shop they had a surprise for us. While exploring the very top rooms up in the roof they found a lady's walking stick parasol. It had been wedged between the rafters and had obviously been there for many years. It's condition was very fragile indeed, and as it was moved the fine lacework

75

fringing the canopy started to disintegrate. The handle and main body was made from cane, and the cane had been decorated with branded crosses down its entire length.

Who had placed it there and why was anybody's guess. Unfortunately we did not try any psycometry on it, something I regret immensely. It looked Victorian in date and would have been quite an expensive item, so why leave it behind? Paul has lived around the area of the shop for many years and told us there was once another street that ran along the back of the existing property called Offal Street, due to the fact there were butchers and fishmongers along there. He also added that the people who once lived in houses above the shops facing the main street were slightly better off than those living in the street behind. He added that many years ago the buildings had been on fire and extensively damaged. While on his walk round with Andy, Paul also picked up on a man with breathing problems. He said he got the feeling the man had been bedridden.

Now we were ready to start the vigils. Andy, Mark, and Paul, started in the rooms upstairs to the left. Gill and Matt decided to try some glass divination downstairs. While Lewis and myself took on the rooms upstairs to the right, downstairs Gill and Matt started asking out for spirits to contact them by moving the glass. There was the odd sound, but the glass remained stationary. They then tried table tipping to see if that would work but again there was no response. The only unusual activity they reported were the noises and the video camera switching itself off, something it had not done before. Meanwhile Andy, Mark, and Paul, were getting activity. They all heard a child's footsteps very close to them, and then a door they had closed suddenly swung open. Thinking this could have been a coincidence they shut the door firmly, so firmly Lewis and myself heard it next door, but within minutes the door opened again. Then Marks video camera switched itself off twice, and they also saw lights above Mark while he was concentrating on filming. As for Lewis and myself, it has to be said we got very little paranormal activity, a few knocks and thuds but these could have been caused by the lads next door. It was still early in the investigation so we were still in a positive mood. During a short break it was decided to take a small table upstairs into the room that was so active for Andy's group, just to see if the spirits in there would move the glass in answer to questions. Lewis and myself went onto a separate floor to see what would happen being close to the séance but not actively involved in it. Although there was contact during the séance with spirits, the group were not 100% convinced. There is a point that all of us reach, especially when carrying out glass divination, when we become suspicious of one another, it is part of our makeup. We want to believe, but that little voice inside our head is saying, somebody around this table is moving the glass. I had decided that after this investigation I would not take part in any more glass divination circles in any future investigations. I want people to come on investigations unafraid to say, no I think that is wrong, don't just go along with something simply because that's what everyone else is doing. Anyway, close to the séance Lewis and myself were hearing, and seeing some strange things, muffled conversations and strange streaking lights.

The conversations could have been the people close to us, but as for the lights, that was a puzzle.

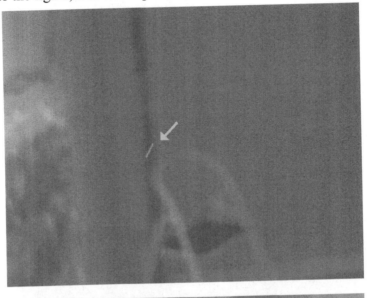

These strange lights have been seen by more than one person.

As I sat there I became aware of someone close to me. I knew Lewis was on the far side of the room so it wasn't him. Then I felt a hand stroke the side of my face, a cold hand but at the same time very gentle. It startled me and Lewis instantly shone a light across at me, but there was nothing to be seen. In fact I was not the only person to have the hand stroke their face, Paul also experienced it. It was time for another break and chat about the investigation so far. Things seemed to be building slowly, you could feel the energy between the team increasing. All of us were at the point where we were expecting something to happen at any moment, it's a great feeling. I decided to go walkabout with my camera. For some reason the night vision video lighting had been playing up all night. I wasn't sure if I had recorded anything other than sound. That's the trouble with infrared, from behind the camera looking through the lens it's daylight, but from in front it's pitch black. It was a good job I decided to check the lighting gear as it had failed completely. I managed to cobble some wires together and switched the power from battery to mains supply, good job we weren't filming outside. While I was alone I decided to take some still shots in the dark. Well you never know what you will see on the photo. I was certainly unprepared for what I was about to photograph. I had taken about six shots with my camera when I spotted something on one of them. I wasn't sure just what it was so I said nothing to anyone that night. When I got the photo on the computer screen I got the shock of my life. There in the corner of the empty room stood a figure of what appeared to be a man with his arms folded, just looking at me. A cold shiver ran down my spine as I thought back to the room and the night's investigation, if we had only known how close we were.

Back to the investigation in hand and people were thinking another séance may be a good idea. To be honest I was not keen, but the consensus was go for it, so that's what we did. During the séance Lewis and myself came in for a bit of stick, apparently the spirits were not pleased with us and the way we were talking about them.

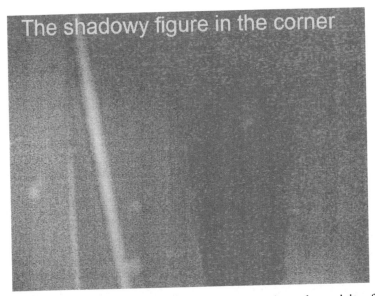

The shadowy figure in the corner

One interesting part to the séance came when the spirit of the previous owner said there was a lost document that needed to be found. What it was and where it could be found was not forthcoming, he did however say the family would find it soon. The séance was the last thing we did during this vigil, and after it had ended we sat around for a while discussing the nights events. It seemed those attending had enjoyed the experience and were glad they had attended. We had just one more vigil at the shop to do, but unfortunately I would not be there due to the fact I was giving a talk with Lewis on the same night. Ken, Tessie, Merlyn and Colin, would be there along with Andy, Mark, Kevin, and some of the family who own the property. Ken gave me the report on the nights investigation.

After a chat about the property's activity the group went upstairs to see what would happen. The mediums and sensitive members of the group tried to contact the spirits within the building. We knew the owners wanted to try to contact the spirit of Richard, he had died some years earlier and was the owner of the shop. The reason I wanted new people to be on the vigil was the existing people knew about Richard. As I have said before, even knowing a small amount about an investigation can, and does, cloud your thoughts. You may have the best intentions in mind but your prior knowledge defeats the exercise. Here is how things went.

The group experienced some strong paranormal activity, including objects falling to the floor. A steel rod fell to the floor as people entered an upper room. This bar had been leaning against a chimneybreast and had been there on previous investigations and had not moved. In fact if you look back at the previous photo you can see it. Ken filmed orbs moving around the assembled group, usually after questions had been asked, coincidence?

After some time upstairs the group went down into the shop to perform a séance. Seven people sat around the table so the energy would have been good. Almost immediately the glass started to move in answer to questions. Kevin asked if the spirit moving the glass was Richard, and to move towards one of his sons if it was. The glass remained motionless. Other names were tried, but still the glass remained still. Andy asked if the spirit knew the sons, after a long pause the glass moved towards one of them. The son in question asked if he had known the spirit while it had been alive, very slowly the glass moved towards him as a sign that he had. They tried some more names and eventually struck on the correct person. The son then asked if the spirit had followed him abroad on a recent trip, again the glass moved. Should he go abroad on the trip planned soon? The movement of the glass was slow and deliberate, "Yes" came the answer. Several other questions were asked and all were answered positively. The spirit then said that it was the son's one and only guide. Kevin then asked if there were any other spirits with them, the glass moved swiftly to answer "Yes". Over the course of the next few questions it was apparent they were now talking to a child called Melanie, a blonde little girl with Irish parents. This little girl has been contacted before on earlier vigils.

This séance was taxing on many of the group and slowly the new people attending drifted away to explore the other areas within the building. While the main séance continued, Andy and Ken were convinced that a spirit that the séance was now picking up on was

81

lying to them. Whoever it was seemed to be moving around the building, Andy and Ken went on the prowl with the night vision to try to track the spirits movements. This was more difficult than they had at first thought so they stopped the pursuit and decided to perform small vigils with Tessie, Ken and Colin in different locations, and boy did this have the desired affect. Tessie, Colin, and Ken, decided to go down into the cellar and see what would happen. Almost immediately Tessie became uneasy with its atmosphere. What followed was a light show of brilliant light rods flashing across a wall in the cellar. They seem to be a few inches in length, and as Tessie said, as bright as a welding light. The three of them searched for a source but could find nothing. Ken filmed the whole thing which lasted several minutes, it then stopped as abruptly as it had started. Ken, Tessie, Merlyn and Colin then climbed the stairs to the upper rooms to see if things up there were as active. Apart from the sound of a girls voice which as Colin so rightly pointed out could have come from the street below, Merlyn was the only one who had strong contact with a spirit. The spirit of a young girl made herself known to her, could this be the owner of the voice Colin had heard? Merlyn also had contact with a spirit energy that knocked her off her feet. A spirit of this type is rear, and normally does things for attention rather than malice. Unfortunately the reason for this attack was not forthcoming.

The vigil downstairs had ended and the investigation finished quietly. A few weeks later I arranged to go over and talk to the owners to see if I could get some background history on the shop. We had the paranormal evidence but did it fit the known facts?

The family were extremely helpful to me during the interview, and I would also like to thank them for allowing us to do the investigations in the first place. The shop we investigated goes back to the late 1890's, possibly even earlier. There were fishmongers, greengrocers, drapers, and furniture shops in abundance along the streets in those days. In fact you name it and there was probably a shop selling it somewhere along the street. It was a community that didn't just help each other, they relied on each other, in ways we can only look back on with admiration and respect. Our little shop was no different to all the rest, supplying practical items for people who needed quality goods they knew would last. Over the years it had been a drapers and a wardrobe dealers, and then in 1928 it seems to have joined forces with its neighbour and became a Clothiers, Boot Factors, and Wardrobe Dealers. Some records do not survive, but it seems the little shop has sold clothing for many years. The main, and indeed dominant figure of the investigation we carried out, was the senior member of the family concerned. He had worked in the shop from the age of sixteen, until his untimely death at the age of forty nine. Some people do a job of work day in day out and are glad when they can get away to do other things, not so in this case, this man lived for the shop. He knew the job back to front and inside out, he also knew his customers just as well. Remember what I said about community spirit? Well this shop had it. People would pop in even if they didn't want to buy anything, just to have a chat. Eventually the whole family became involved working all hours, it was a successful business. But as with all things in life, change is inevitable, and success isn't everlasting, even if we want it to be. After the death of the man at forty nine the family carried on, working hard to survive in an ever changing world that decided cost was more important than quality. They were successful for a good few years, but finally decided enough was enough. The business closed and the shop became empty. Then strange sounds and feelings started to be heard and felt by people entering the building, and that's where I came in. Over the years I have noted certain patterns of events, triggered in this case by the start of renovations. It seems that energy and spirits are disturbed by such activity. At this point it is important to know that the feeling among the family members, understandably, is one of regret, regret at not being able to continue with the business. With this in their minds and the increasing activity, it's no wonder the family's first thoughts turned to their lost loved one.

Going back through the investigations, you can see that there is trapped residual energy that has indeed been released. Names and dates are of people who have been connected with the building in some way or another. Residual energy is not spirit, it's ghost, something that is left behind after the event. The spirits that visit the shop are fewer in number, possibly three at the most. I say visit with good reason, these spirits visit on occasions only, they do not inhabit the shop. I think the spirit of the owner is just watching, interested to see what things are being done. Remember this, spirits do not judge us by our actions. Whatever the future holds for the family and the shop, it's they who decide what is done and when.

I wish them every success in their endeavours.

Abington Park Museum

Here is a special investigation that was done in collaboration with the local Northampton paranormal group.

Emma Whiteman, formed The Northampton Paranormal Group at the beginning of 2007. To her surprise the membership of the group shot up to over twenty five in a matter of weeks. I knew Emma before the group started so when she asked me if I would like to join them on some investigations I agreed. I could not become a full time member due to my own investigations and writing taking up most of my time. However, I am a great advocate of groups working together. There is far too much, "we are better than you" going on in the paranormal world today. If you are a true investigator you will welcome help from others. It's the same with mediums, I can do this so I am better than you, how childish is that. I have seen this attitude so many times. Emma knows I enjoy working with others, and sharing knowledge is a fantastic way of bonding with people.

One investigation she asked me to cover with her group was at Abington Park Museum in Northampton. The house had never been investigated before so this would be really interesting. The museum itself is housed in the manor house which was built around 1500 by John Bernard. Its hammerbeam roof and oak panelling was a main feature of the great hall. The house was also once the home to Shakespeare's granddaughter, Elizabeth Bernard, who is buried in the nearby church of St Peter and St Paul. After several generations of Bernard's, the house was sold in 1669 to William Thursby, for £13,750. The house then passed to John Harvey in 1736, a distant relative of William Thursby. Interestingly, John Harvey was required to add the Thursby name to his under the terms of the will. Successive generations altered the house enlarging it as their needs required. Finally in 1841 the house ceased to be a family home and was sold for £88,000. The house was bought by Lewis Loyd, a banker living in Overstone. He let the property in 1845 and it became a private mental asylum.

The asylum closed in 1892 and the manor, along with 20 acres were given to Northampton by Lady Wantage, granddaughter of Lewis Lloyd. Part of the house was opened to the public and used as a café. Gradually other rooms were opened and used to house museum collections and so on, then in 1964 electric lighting was installed. The building was finally restored in 1994 and reopened to the public. It now houses many fine collections from around Northamptonshire, including Northampton's military history, both home and abroad, and some exquisite 16th century oak panelling.

Before we go into the details of the investigation it is important to know some of the people attending. Emma had some really interesting people within her group who were intent on finding out the truth about ghosts and spirits. There are too many to name here, but I will do my best to pick out some people who have gone on to do interesting paranormal investigations. Ken Hayes, (Photographic and technical), Teresa Neil, (Technical and historical research), Mandy & Colin Knight, (Spiritual and experimental techniques), Lewis Dellar, (Technical and Training in Parapsychology), and me, (Old git in glasses). These, along with fifteen others attended the museum investigation. Emma, with husband Mark and her father Denis in support, had planned the investigation like a military operation. It had to be done in this way due to the size of location and number of people attending. We would have from 11.00 pm until 4.00 am to do a full investigation. Emma decided to split the people into five groups of four. Each group would spend thirty minutes in a given location then move onto the next. She wanted people to get as much information from the museum in the time allocated, this was the only feasible way to do it. Unfortunately this meant a hectic start for myself and Ken Hayes who were trying to set up video and sound recording equipment in several locations. We could not set things up before the allocated time so we had just half an hour to cover the whole building. Meanwhile Emma was briefing the others, along with a representative of the museum who would oversee the investigation. Training parapsychologist, Lewis Dellar, would be there to give a balanced viewpoint on any paranormal activity experienced. People were allocated to groups and the groups were sent to their start locations. At eleven thirty all was set for the start. I was in Emma's group along with Gill and Carol, we were as keyed up as the rest of the groups.

Now if you have never done an investigation in a museum before, let me tell you what to avoid, reflections from glass display cabinets, mannequins , creaking floorboards and walkie-talkies. Unfortunately we had all of these in abundance so this wasn't going to be easy.

Our first location was a corridor made from glass display units housing mannequins dressed in Victorian clothing. With all the lighting off the darkness was intense, almost claustrophobic. Once everyone had settled into their first location quietness descended. All our senses were heightened, ready to register the slightest sound, visual movement or temperature drop .

Gill and myself studying the structural detail within the museum. You can learn a lot from simply reading a building.

The seventeenth Century staircase

Northampton Paranormal Group
At Abington Park Museum In Northampton
On The 15th Of September 2007

Apart from some shadowy movement and cold spots our first location was interesting, but slightly disappointing. This isn't surprising. When starting such a large investigation anticipation is high. I don't care who you are, you will always be affected by the people around you when emotions are high.

The word came over the radios for us to move to the next location. This is when we realised the biggest problem investigating the museum, echoing corridors and creaking floorboards. You could hear people moving about in other groups all over the building. Emma put the word out for people to stay quiet and to remain as still as possible, people were reporting hearing noises that were not paranormal, just people wandering about. We did however see some strange lighting under a doorway by the older stairway, and we knew there was nobody on the other side of the door. The light we saw looked like someone walking on the other side of the doorway carrying a candle, you could see the movement. Things started to warm up in a paranormal way when one group reported hearing a door open or close, close to them. Another heard whispering, and the medium working with us, Andrew Garley, was picking up on several spirits in various locations.

St. Peter & St. Paul, Abington, Northampton
The Manor House is just visible to the right.

After a short break we set off again. This time we climbed the elegant seventeenth century staircase leading from the great hall. This is an atmospheric area and obviously one that has seen its fair share of traffic over the years. This in mind I had set up a night vision video camera recording any movement from the top of the third flight. It had recorded each groups movements on the staircase during the entire investigation, interestingly, at least one person from each group paused and looked down the staircase from this third flight. Andrew Garley said later that he could feel a spirit energy on the staircase at that point. I took time out to sit quietly on my own at the top of the staircase. It has a calm, protective, warm feeling, as though you are being observed by a friendly spirit. It was a pleasant experience and one I will remember for some time. Our group then entered a room at the end of a corridor leading from the staircase which had American Indian artefacts in glass cases. It was in here that we heard tapping on the glass cases, in answer to questions. There was also a sense of unbalance, especially when closing your eyes. Lewis said this could have been due to an uneven floor, common in buildings of this age.

Here is something for you to remember, ninety percent of incidents that occur on investigations are not paranormal. They can be answered in logical terms. It's the ten percent that you cannot answer in logical terms that you are looking for. I know Lewis wanted to move among the groups during this investigation to get an overall picture of what was going on, and pinpoint the hotspots, but due to the nature of the building and the noise created by people walking about this was not practical. The next piece of paranormal activity to be witnessed by our group was in a room that is not normally open to the public. Will, the member of staff from the museum, decided to join our group at this point, just at the right time. We were sitting quietly and had decided to ask the spirits to give us a sign. Immediately there was a loud bang from the floor beneath Will's chair, so forceful we could feel the vibration across the other side of the room. We asked again. Yet again the bang came loud and clear. Later I asked if anyone else had had a similar experience. Lewis's group had experienced the same phenomena, and even Lewis could not find a logical reason for the noise. There were central heating pipes running around the room, and they were warm, but the sound was not floorboards creaking against each other. Lewis had even caught the phenomena on video. When I watched the footage it was even louder than our group had remembered.

We had had a difficult and demanding investigation. Even with the number of people attending the vigil, Emma and her supporting team had done a great job. However, I feel if another investigation was planned, it should have the number of people attending kept down to around five or six. There are rooms and floors within the museum that are yet to be explored. I for one hope I am at the next investigation. As for the conclusion, is the museum haunted ? Yes, but in a subtle way. If you were not looking for it you would probably not even notice.

The museum's staff were very helpful when I went back to find out about the people who had once lived in the house, and changes that had been made to the building during its history. It is better to do this after doing a paranormal investigation. Prior knowledge of a place has a huge influence on your thought process when you are trying to pick up on spirit contact. In fact I would go as far as to say it invalidates any information you think you may have received. Unconsciously your brain uses the knowledge you have to make sense of what is happening around you. Let me give you an example. If you know a murder took place at a specific location, when you go to the location you are automatically waiting for something to happen, you can't help but think about what you have learnt.

Going into an investigation cold is of paramount importance, and only then will you seek out any true paranormal activity. If you validate the information received you have done a true investigation.

Kirlian Photography

Now let us delve into new territory. A friend of mine has used Kirlian photography in the past as a tool for pinpointing possible ailments within the body, I will explain how it works in a moment. She is now testing this photographic process to see if it is possible to use it within the spiritual and paranormal fields of investigation. Before I introduce her let's take a close look at what Kirlian photography is, and how it works.

Kirlian Photography came about by sheer chance back in 1939. A Russian electrician, Semyon Kirlian, was working in the city hospital of Krasnodas. He was watching a physiotherapy machine in operation when a spark jumped between an electrode and the patients skin. Kirlian wondered how the spark might appear if it were photographed. Being a part time inventor he built a device to test his theory. He burnt his hand on his first test but when he processed the film he saw his hand surrounded by a halo, similar to that reportedly seen by people who say they can see a persons aura. This new electro photography involves putting a film on top of a flat metal plate, then placing an object on the film and photographing it while an electrical charge is passed through the plate. This photographic process will produce auras that vary in colour, size and shape when animate or inanimate subjects are used. Since its discovery the process has been adapted and is now widely used in many fields, Medicine, Psychology, Agriculture, Criminology, Iridology and Reflexology, Hands-on Healing, Acupuncture, Touch for Health, Shiatsu and Stress Management.

As you can see there are unlimited applications for this process. It seems to be able to show a persons bio energy field. Your energy field is affected by the chemical makeup within your body at any given time. These chemicals change when we become unwell or feel anger or stress. Basically all living things have an energy field emanating from them, with this photographic technique we can see it. Tear a leaf in half and place the torn half in the Kirlian machine and you will see the whole leaf, the energy from the missing half is still visible. Doctors have done tests with

93

amputees with similar results, the missing limb shows up as an energy field. Now you know a little more about the process let's go into the interview.

Mandy Knight, or Merlyn to her friends, lives in Rushden, Northamptonshire. She is a highly intelligent and spiritually aware person, who likes to push the boundaries of subjects she comes into contact with. Along with husband Colin, they both spend a good deal of time trying to find out about spirit communication with the living. Kirlian photography is another tool that may be able to answer some questions.

Mandy attended a healing class in Manchester in April 2001. While there she met a woman called Amanda Baker, a sister for 25 years at the A&E department of the North Manchester Hospital. Amanda bought her Kirlian camera along with her to the class. Mandy had never seen one before and was intrigued. She had seen aura cameras before where the head and shoulders are photographed, these are hugely expensive pieces of equipment that Mandy could never see herself ever using. The lady with the Kirlian camera was offering before and after photographs in conjunction with healing work. The technique being used was fingertip photography. You put your hand into a black sleeve and place your fingertips onto a film. An electrical current is passed through a plate below the film which takes a recording of the energy output from your fingertips, the camera has no eye as such. You move your fingers back down the film about twenty millimetres and repeat the process up to a further three times. Each time you move your fingers you are asked to think of a different emotion. Your emotions should send out varying energy levels which should appear on the photo. Mandy had her fingertips photographed and had some unusual results, there were someone else's fingertips with hers. After the healing class she had another photo taken that showed these extra fingertips again much brighter and larger, the extra prints were that of a man. This photography immediately fascinated Mandy, and in her own words she said,"I had to know more". All this happened in 2001, and the lady who took the camera to the healing class is now a good friend and has taught her a lot about the subject. About eighteen months ago Mandy finally purchased her own Kirlian camera and has been experimenting with it ever since.

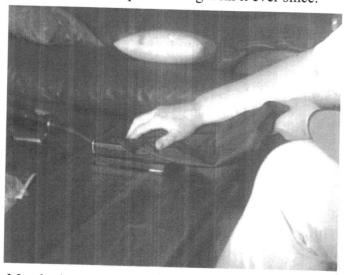

Mandy demonstrating how the fingertips are placed on the photographic plate.

Once you start looking at Kirlian photography, you suddenly realise how vast the subject is. Mandy told me that she has spent seven years learning from her friend, and seeing how the Kirlian camera works in a medical diagnostic and spiritual way. The diagnosis is only a way of informing a person about potential problems that the process picks up on. You need medical training and experience of using the Kirlian camera before you can attempt this. Similarly, the spiritual side to this, analysing emotional and spiritual energy, also takes training and an understanding of how the body's energy naturally flows. Readings on the camera show up as different colours and patterns for different states of being. On the next few pages are some photos taken with the camera showing the aura around the fingertips. The pictures in this book are, as you can see, in black and white. This does detract from the original image, and I suggest that if you have access to the internet you type in Kirlian Photography. There you will see more examples in full colour.

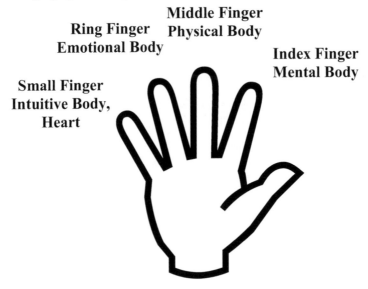

Middle Finger
Physical Body

Ring Finger
Emotional Body

Index Finger
Mental Body

Small Finger
Intuitive Body,
Heart

Finger placement and thoughts

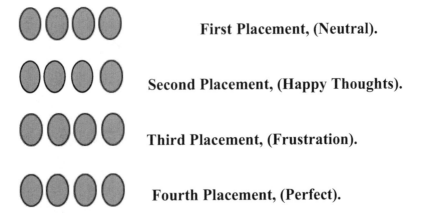

First Placement, (Neutral).

Second Placement, (Happy Thoughts).

Third Placement, (Frustration).

Fourth Placement, (Perfect).

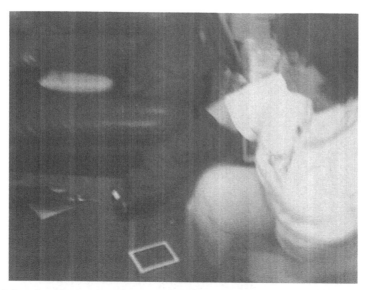

Mandy demonstrating the black glove attached to the camera.

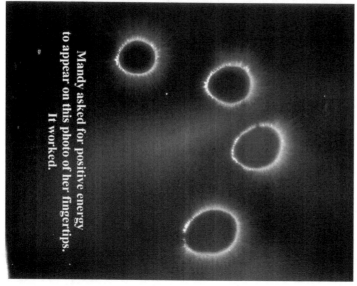

Mandy asked for positive energy to appear on this photo of her fingertips. It worked.

Knowing your thought processes can alter your psychic energy, Mandy tried to influence the photograph, and succeeded. A few years ago Mandy and a group of friends toured Egypt

97

visiting temples at Karnak, Abydos and Dendera. Shortly afterwards she had her fingertips photographed. Some years later she tried an experiment, she tried to picture herself back at Dendera and tried to bring back the emotions of that day. The next two photos show the results.

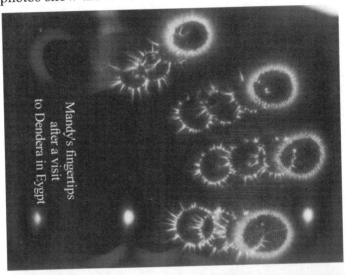

Mandy's fingertips after a visit to Dendera in Eygpt

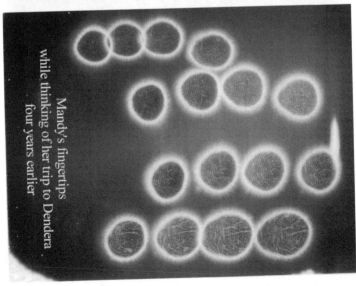

Mandy's fingertips while thinking of her trip to Dendera four years earlier

The energy a person can develop simply by thought is remarkable. But what else can give out this kind of energy?

This is what the energy of an egg looks like when photographed

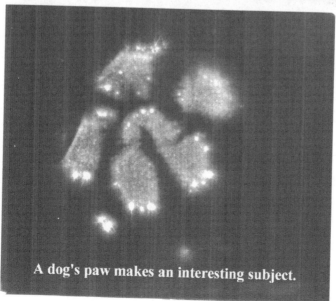

A dog's paw makes an interesting subject.

The first attempt at photographing my fingertips resulted in this strange image,

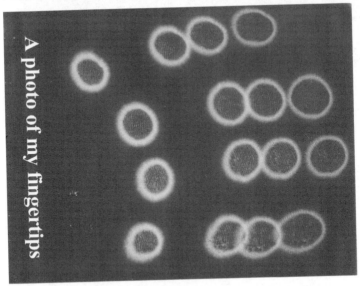

A photo of my fingertips

I had to see what results Mandy would get from the camera on my fingertips. Nothing too strange there, well I am a ghost detective.

This type of photographic analysis could be successfully incorporated into a paranormal investigation. As Mandy explained to me during the interview, a before and after photo could be used to see if your energy levels decrease or are infused during spirit contact.

Mandy went on to tell me that when people visit places like Dendera, or Karnak, they are told the history of the place, but if you were to just pause for a moment and take in the atmosphere; you would find the energy of the people who once lived and worshiped within these temples still exists. Allow this energy to flow into you and you will be empowered. This energy never leaves you, and years later you will be able to call on it , and as you saw in the photos, it will resurface.

Mandy is one of those people who are not afraid to experiment with things. It's all too easy to go with the flow and take things easy. You should question and test things for yourself, it's how we learn. What this photographic method teaches us more than anything else, it's that an accident can, and often does, open doors to new ways of thinking.

Before the interview ended I asked Mandy the percentage question. On the average investigation what percentage would she say was down to natural causes, and what percentage was down to paranormal. Her answer? 95% natural, and 5% paranormal.

Kirlian photography is a subject that requires further investigation and experimentation. With the help from people like Mandy who knows where it will lead us. I have only scratched the surface of the subject in this book. I hope you have learnt that there are techniques being used today that will give us further pieces to the paranormal jigsaw.

Parapsychology and Science

Some may ask what place parapsychology and science have in a book about ghost and spirit investigation. The answer? They are a vital part of any investigation. Let me explain. You cannot investigate the paranormal with a blinkered approach, that will get you nowhere. Imagine going into someone's house and telling them that everything that they hear and see is paranormal. Not only would this be untrue, but totally irresponsible. We have a duty to anyone asking for our help to answer their questions honestly. If there is a draught creating a cold spot, say so. If there are rodents in the loft creating noises at night, explain this to the client. Too many people are encouraged to believe in the paranormal by people who have a vested interest in perpetuating such stories. Thankfully we tell people the truth, if its paranormal we will say so and pursue the investigation, if its' not we will explain how we know this and bring the investigation to a close.

Lewis Dellar is training in parapsychology and is looking for the same answers we are, he approaches the subject from a scientific angle. I have first hand experience of ghosts and spirits and approach investigations from that angle. Together we have formed an alliance that helps us investigate reports of paranormal activity effectively and successfully.

I asked Lewis when he first became interested in investigating the paranormal. He explained that when he was about nine or ten years of age his father, a military man based at Wootton Barracks in Northampton, left the army after sixteen years and started up a painting and decorating business. He was working at the school for the blind in Northampton during one half term. The building was horseshoe shaped and Lewis's father was working in one end. He could clearly see someone staring at him through a window from the other side of the courtyard, in the other wing of the building. Thinking it was probably someone helping the site supervisor he thought no more of it. The site supervisor then came into the room and Lewis father quizzed him about the other person he had seen looking at him from the window opposite. He was informed that they were the only two people in the building and there was nobody in that part of the school. Lewis's father was a bit miffed at this and shrugged it off as a mistake on his part. Then over time he saw other things that he could not explain. He was a man who did not believe in ghosts, but had no explanation for the things he had seen. This sparked an interest in Lewis to find the truth behind such things. He has always wanted to know the answer to unanswered questions. Parapsychology is one way Lewis feels able to investigate, not just paranormal questions, but other questions that have perplexed him and others for many years. He said he has always wanted to go and investigate places he was not allowed to. The locked door in the castle, the bricked up tunnel, the hidden room, and so on. Explorers need to go further than anyone else and Lewis now has the chance to pull all his interests together, history, archaeology, and science, all into one package.

Lewis started his Higher National Diploma course in August 2007 to get a form of qualification to get started on the Parapsychology course. He has completed some non academic courses to get an understanding of what was required. Once he has completed the High National Diploma he then has to do a degree in Psychology which is a four year part time course. Normally this would be a two year course, unfortunately Lewis needs to work full time so he can only study part time, thus increasing the time needed to take the course. This done Lewis hopes to work as a Medical Psychologist while studying for a PHD in Parapsychology, taking another four years. I asked Lewis what his final aim was. Lecturing in Parapsychology, while investigating the paranormal full time is what he wants to do.

I then asked him how he sees the future of Parapsychology, joining forces with paranormal investigation? Or would they always be at odds with one another.. He said he can always see people in both camps having fixed ideas, too set in their views to want to join forces and this will always be a problem. However, we are constantly trying to build the bridges between the tested theories that we do understand , to the ones that are just beyond our understanding. That in essence is Parapsychology, and the essence of every science. Pushing the boundaries of theories and testing them to try to find comparative results, if they check out people are happy with that. Lewis then quoted a saying which is very true, "To the believer no truth is necessary, and to the non believer no proof is enough".

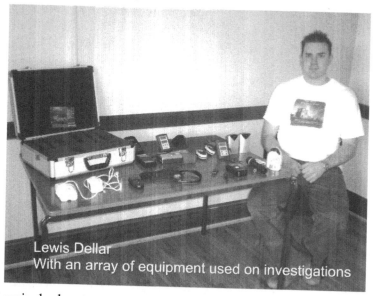

Lewis Dellar
With an array of equipment used on investigations

Lewis had set out an array of equipment he uses during investigations. You may recognise some of the equipment in the photo, but in case you do not I asked him to explain what the equipment was and how it is used.

We started with a piece of equipment from the centre of the table called an EMF meter. This is used to measure electro magnetic fields, natural and otherwise. In houses all electrical goods give off magnetic field energy. The meter gives an audible and visual reading that lets you know what strength of magnetic field you are being subjected to. There is evidence to suggest that high exposure to EMF for any length of time can induce headaches, nausea, itchy skin, and the feeling of being watched. Some of the new EMF meters are so sensitive they can pick up the magnetic field given out by a person. Using these in an investigation is not advisable, because if you get a group of people in a room and you are trying to get EMF readings from that room, it will be picking up on them and not on the room itself. More expensive is not always better. It is surprising how many things around us can affect us in an emotional way without us ever knowing they are there. At least when investigating with this type of equipment we can say if the problem is likely to be normal as opposed to paranormal. I asked Lewis to explain what some of the other things he had on the table did. EVP recorders, tape and digital. These record Electronic Voice Phenomena, voices you cannot hear naturally. Even with these it seems the old tape versions of recorder work better than the digital one's. Again this could be due to the magnetic energy being picked up.. I have personally heard recorded voices, music and animal sounds that could not be heard by the people in the room at the time. These sounds seem to be set at a different frequency to the ones we normally hear, but when played back on a tape or digital recorder they change into a frequency we can hear. This is a useful tool to use on investigations. Other equipment Lewis had on the table included indoor and outdoor thermometers and hydro thermometers. With these thermometers you can measure the temperatures within, or around a building, and also measure the humidity within a building, useful when people are getting orb photos. Too much moisture within a building will give you orbs that are reflections of minute water droplets in the atmosphere.

Lewis also has a pressure censor. Basically what this does is measure the pressure within a particular room. If you have a house with a history of doors opening and closing by themselves, sometimes this is due to alternating pressure within rooms, when one door is closed it causes another to open in a different part of the house. With this meter you can monitor the pressure level in the room to see if it is this causing the door to open or close.

Lewis then moved on to explain about another meter he uses called a cell censor

Lewis demonstrating the Cell Censor

The cell censor measures RF, or radio frequency. If you were to hear voices or heard music during an investigation this meter could rule out radio signals as a cause. Radio waves are in many things we use on a day to day basis, mobile phones being one of the most common. Primarily these meters are used to see if a device is giving off safe levels of RF.

I asked Lewis what would be the best possible way for him to start an investigation, if he were given ample time to set up his equipment. He explained that on most investigations he was invited to, he wasn't given any time to monitor the location during the day and night. If he was able to go into a building, set up the equipment, and record readings over twenty four hours, this would give a range of readings he knew were normal for that location. If you then go into the location to do an investigation, and readings went outside the set range while activity was being recorded, he could then say that while activity was present a given electronic reading was higher than normal.

If you have a group of people experiencing paranormal activity and nobody is monitoring them, or the location they are in, then the scientific community will simply dismiss the evidence as meaningless. That is why we must join forces, not just to find out if there is life after death, some of us already know the answer to that, we need to go further. We need to explore the link between the spirit world and our own. We also need to tap into the wealth of knowledge that is recorded naturally in the world around us.

Finally, I asked Lewis, as a percentage, what activity on investigations he has done is down to natural causes, and what activity is due to paranormal causes. His answer was 98% natural and 2% paranormal. Interestingly we are only 8% apart, but it's that little percentage, the golden percentage, that holds the key to many unanswered questions.

Spiritual Awareness

Judy C works with me on a regular basis, and it is to her we turn for this interview. People often ask, how do we become spiritually aware? There is no easy answer to this, so in an attempt to help you get an understanding of the subject, this interview is an example of one persons' journey to their own spiritual awareness.

As with so many people who have had a lifelong interest in the paranormal, Judy first realised she could hear things at a very early age. She would lie in bed and hear footsteps along corridors, and hear doors opening and closing in rooms close by. At the time she was told it was all in her imagination, but she knew it wasn't. Then at the age of eighteen she saw a figure standing at the foot of her bed, not a relative, or threatening in any way, just a figure that stood for a moment and then faded. Judy felt as though the figure was there as a comforting sign, letting her know there was someone watching out for her. The sighting was just before Judy was about to start college, a coincidence? Judy believes there is no such thing as a coincidence. Everything that happens to you in life is meant for a reason. During her younger years her spiritual thought had yet to be developed and learning a profession came first.

Life doesn't always allow us to do what we would like to do, and for Judy her professional career gave little time to sit and ponder on the deeper questions we would all like answers to. As time went on she had additional responsibilities with a family and all the work that that brings. However, she did find time to do a little reading, that kept the willingness to learn more about her own spirituality alive. Later on she found herself with a little more time and she began to read more and study the subject of spirit in depth. She also started to visit a spiritualist church to gain experience and discuss the experiences of others. Over the next few years Judy also joined various groups who sat in circle and tried to contact the spirit world. All this time she was adding to her knowledge, I call this being time served. There are no quick routes to knowledge, you have to go through the lessons before you learn how to help yourself, then, and only then, are you in a position to help others.

Being spiritually aware you tend to find your own heightened gifts, whether they are clairvoyance, mediumistic, or healing. There are a large range of gifts, some of which you may possess and some you may not. Judy's gift's are spiritual healing, and she is spiritually mediumistic, not a spiritualist medium, there is a difference. To be a spiritualist you need a religious belief, but to be spiritual you need to believe in the continuation of the human spirit lasting after death. But they are the same thing I hear you cry. No they are not, and here is why. A spiritualist believes in the soul of a person being sacred. To transcend into heaven you have to be pure of heart and without sin, hell awaits those who fail and eternal torment awaits you. A spiritual person believes in the inner spirit that transcends the physical life and goes on to exist in a realm where anything and everything is possible, still linked with the people and places we know.

I told you this wasn't going to be easy. I am trying to help you understand something that has taken, not only Judy, but many others, including myself, many years to understand.

You do not need to be religious to believe in an existence after the physical life has ended. I am not saying spiritualists are wrong or right, it is something the individual needs to have total faith in, If you believe it, and have total faith in it, then you live your life to that way of thinking.

To get back to the gifts spiritual awareness can enhance, Judy's healing gift is something I asked her to explain a little further. Healing is the transference of energy from one person to another. With hands-on healing you need to tune in to the person who has asked for your help. Usually you would place your hands on their shoulders to form an initial form of contact, the energy is then transferred from the centre of the palms of the healer. The healer picks up on the part of the patients body that requires attention, usually without consciously thinking, they are simply guided to the point. It is like an intuitive knowledge picked up from the person

110

asking to be helped. Some healers use two gifts at once, healing, and clairvoyance, picking up from the patient where the pain or ailment is located. This method can cause the healer to actually feel the pain of the patient. To get to this level the healer must be linked into the patient in such a way that they shut out everything else around them and become totally focused on the feelings being transferred.

I hope you can see from this that healing, along with other gifts, spiritual or spiritualist, takes time to learn. You cannot read a book and think you can do the job. Here is a quote from Judy, "Reading can merely point you in a direction you think you would like to travel, but the best pointer is the feeling you get from within yourself".

It must be stressed at this point that spiritual healing is not, and never should be, used as a replacement for medical treatment. It should only enhance medical treatment.

I asked Judy what she looks for when investigating somewhere for the first time. She explained that unlike many people with us on any given investigation, she needs to be on her own for a while. If you are setting up equipment or doing tests you cannot be focused on the spirit side of things. This is also true for myself. Trying to make sure everyone attending an investigation gets the best possible chance to experience something takes my attention away from the main reason I am there. I know the investigation calms down after a while and we can all focus on things, but it would be nice not to have the organisational worries in the back of my mind. Judy describes the feelings she gets on entering a building that has spirit activity, as similar to the ones you get when house hunting. You walk into a house and instinctively know whether you like it or not. That instinctive feeling is what you use when looking for spirit. Judy believes that everyone can experience that feeling, they just block it out, concentrating on their busy lives.

When experiencing true spirit contact people can often be surprised, or even scared, but Judy gets annoyed at people getting hysterical. She feels TV and films have a lot to answer for regarding hysterical behaviour from people on investigations. If she entered a building where she felt threatened in any way she would not continue with the investigation, unless there were people present she could rely upon to give her support if needed. You can be made ill if you are ultra sensitive to something you make contact with that is unpleasant, and I do mean physically ill. Fortunately this does not happen often, but you must be aware of the possibility.

Now, when we talk about spiritual activity on investigations we do not mean knocks, bangs, or footsteps along hallways. These are all residual energy, echoes from the past. What Judy is talking about is direct contact from spirit entity.

I then asked Judy how religious she was, or indeed if she was religious at all. She quoted from a book she had just read. "It's easy to believe in God, because you don't question it you just believe it. It's easy to be an atheist because you just flatten everything. It's the agnostic that is the hardest one to be". In fact Judy was bought up as Church of England, Sunday school, church choir, confirmed, the whole bit. She remembered it as being quite a strict regime. She doesn't feel religious anymore, having thought about the things she has experienced during her life. She does however believe there is good in all of us, and that nobody is born evil. Some people are born mentally ill, or unstable, but not evil or bad. Judy then emphasized the point that a person may not be religious, but they can be deeply spiritual within themselves.

I then asked Judy a question I like to ask everyone who works with me. In percentage terms, what percentage of activity during an investigation is due to natural causes, and what percentage is due to paranormal activity. Answers to this question can be very enlightening. And Judy's answer? 90% natural and 10% paranormal. Judy then added, peoples expectation and imagination can also play a big part in an investigation. The power of suggestion can cause people to smell something, hear something, or even feel something. In some situations when on an investigation the atmosphere can become so tense it only takes the slightest noise to cause a form of hysteria that can spread like wildfire. Screaming, running, and even laugher to release nervous tension are all things I have witnessed. It's interesting to see how people cope in different ways to situations that are unfamiliar. Psychology is something you find yourself studying as you investigate the paranormal.

Judy is experienced in the art of meditation, indeed this goes hand in hand with spirituality. If you can obtain an altered form of consciousness you can then receive communication from the spirit world, if they want you to. Many psychologists theorise about altered states of consciousness, but how many of them have actually experienced it. Judy's advice to anyone wishing to explore their spiritual side is to go to a spiritualist church and ask questions.

I had a discussion with Judy regarding the two main points that have emerged from this book, captured energy, forming recordings of the past that we now know as ghosts and direct communication with spirit by mediums and sensitive's. I believe the captured energy theory will soon be proved, but I doubt that people will ever come to terms with the fact that people can, and do, communicate with spirits. Judy believes that the reason why most people can't pick up on the energy recordings, and spirits, is because we have lost the primitive senses we all once had. We unconsciously block out the senses that would allow us to see and hear so much more. Animals can still see and hear far more than us, you can learn a lot by watching their reactions in so-called haunted places. Stored memories can only be picked up from the location they were released into, but spirits can travel anywhere. Remember this when you are doing investigations of your own, it may help you decide just what type of contact you are getting.

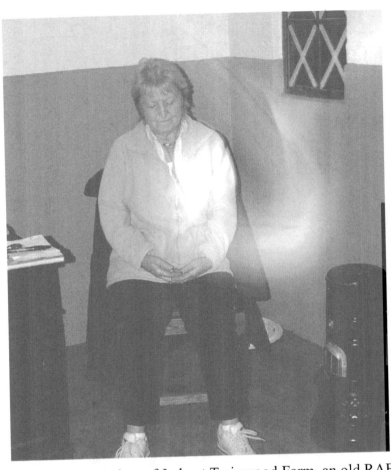

This photo was taken of Judy at Twinwood Farm, an old RAF Station from WWII.

She knew something was going to happen and asked Richard to take the shot. The only lighting in the room was the light from the digital flash camera. The light that surrounded her lit up her clothing and the wall below the window. In my opinion it is one of the best photos of spirit activity I have ever seen.

Conclusions

I am constantly being asked by people, do I believe in ghosts. My answer is yes, ghosts are real. People never ask me if I believe in spirits, simply because they believe ghosts and spirits are one and the same. Having read this book I hope you have learnt that there is a difference between the two. Science will soon be able to verify the existence of ghosts. They will proudly say they have discovered it through years of research. However, it's the countless groups and investigation teams that have strived over the years to gather the information that have really discovered the truth. We are just waiting for science to catch up with us.

As for spirits, this is something science will take longer to accept, if they ever do. To accept that spirits exist they would need to rewrite the laws of physics and add another dimension to our known world. I won't see it in this earthly life, but I will see it in the next.

It's your reaction to that last sentence that tells how far you have travelled from the mainstream way of thinking. If you truly have an open mind you will acknowledge other ways of thinking. Obviously we all have ideas that we have formed over years that govern the way we live our lives. But to keep learning, as we must all do, you need to be shown something new. Never ever stop wanting to learn more about yourself, and the world around you. All the investigations in this book were instigated by people with an insatiable hunger for knowledge. You would not have picked this book up if you did not have that same hunger.

Now let us take a final look at the investigations covered in this book. La Oficina was a delight to investigate, this was mainly due to the welcome we received from the people working there. Our findings were almost totally ghost orientated. I think the energy was released by the atmosphere of uncertainty about the future. The people working in there were worried about things and collectively this affected the atmosphere. We did get names and dates that

115

hopefully someone will be able to shed light on one day. The restaurant was up for sale as we concluded the investigation, and yes it was sad to see people's efforts going to waste. Maybe they are meant to go on to do better things elsewhere, I hope so. People who are prepared to work that hard deserve to succeed

Blisworth Tunnel was a challenge, but I think we rose to it well. Experiencing difficult situations on investigations teaches you how to overcome seemingly impossible tasks. Nature throws some pretty atrocious weather at us from time to time and you soon learn water and electricity don't really like each other, even at low voltage. However, with the help of a good team investigations are always enjoyable, even if you do get extremely wet. During this investigation we picked up on ghost and not spirit. The energy residue from events long ago is still there. We were able to verify the information received, after the event, and we learnt some of the history surrounding the tunnel. All in all I think we succeeded in our investigation, and had a good deal of fun at the same time. At school I hated history with a passion you would not believe, but now I can't learn fast enough. If you ever find yourself at Stoke Bruerne check out the tunnel, it's well worth it.

The haunted house in Kettering has to be one of my all time favourites. Difficult to sort out how to approach it at first due to its complexity. A process of elimination finally found us with a small group of people that the spirits seemed to be happy with, and yes I did say spirits. It was one investigation that had ghost and spirit, a rare event indeed. The family were all aware of the spirits within the property, but the spirits were attracted by the owners more than anyone else. Both of them have had experience of spirits as children and there were more spirits visiting that house than I had ever come across before. We threw everything at the place in an effort to help the spirits move on. When this failed we decided to work with the spirits to try to find out who they were and what it was they wanted.

116

It took a year to finally sort out who the dominant spirits were, this done it seemed they wanted Alan to help them. Frustratingly we could never find out how he was meant to help them, they just kept asking for his help. He was willing to help, but the spirits seemed reluctant to let him know how. The family have moved house now and if history repeats itself I will meet them again soon. These spirits will not give up, and neither will we.

Onto the Bedford shop investigation. Pleasant company and an atmospheric location gave us an investigation to remember. Equipment failure was common here, mainly battery failure. This is a well known phenomenon and one we were ready for. What got to me more than anything else on this investigation was the story of the former owner that developed over our visits, he had died a few years earlier but his spirit was still strong. Call me an old romantic if you like but the more I heard about him the more I liked him. History teaches us that previous generations had their own individual trials and tribulations, poverty and disease being most the prominent among the poor. But through all their troubles there was an undeniable sense of community that we seem to have lost. Today it is all about being the individual, stand out from the crowd and do it to them before they can do it to you. Maybe we should remember those from the past, members of the community that took pride in their work and were unafraid to show it. The owner of the shop we investigated was just such a person, he was a hard working chap and part of a community that has all but disappeared. The shop itself holds many ghosts from the past, but it's only trace energy from them that remains. The spirit of the previous owner is the strongest by far, he visits now and then to see what changes are being made, and to see how the family are coping with difficult decisions. As I have said before in this book, the spirits do not judge us, we live our own lives in our own way, as they did. The shop is similar to many others around the country, moving with the times, and what the family are doing today is part of tomorrows' history. (Don't worry about things you have no control over).

117

There are many spirits watching us every day of our lives . They guide us and help us when things become difficult. It's up to us whether we listen to them or not.

Abington Park Museum. A beautiful location packed with history, you couldn't ask for a better place to investigate. Northampton Paranormal Group had the opportunity to go in and do just that. The short time limit and the size of the location meant that a large number of people were needed to cover as much of it as possible. Large numbers are never ideal but there was no choice in this case. NPG were up to the task and handled the investigation with military precision. The building threw up challenges regarding echoing footsteps and voices but results were achieved. There are memories from the past trapped within its walls, and there are a couple of spirits that were identified, these spirits were not resident but visiting. This means that you could visit the museum several times over a year and only experience spirit on one occasion. I suppose a small investigation would find out more about the spirits in there, but it would need to be an all night investigation something I doubt the museum staff would choose to do. I think the staff at the museum were helpful and patient during and after the investigation, and to be that helpful when you do not believe in the paranormal is to be commended. I learnt a lot about Northampton visiting the museum and I frequently go back to visit and look around.

Now on to the interviews. I wanted to add a little more information to the book to help the reader understand some of the skills used on investigations. I know if you have purchased this book you already have an interest in the subject of ghosts and spirits, the people interviewed have skills that add to the information we can gather on an investigation. If you want to build a house you need the people with the skills to do the job, this holds true with an investigation. My investigations would not be as successful without the help of the people around me. Forget the tight paranormal investigation group, personalities will give them a limited life span. Instead, get to know the people in your area who actively search for the paranormal and call on their help now and then. Judge the skills you require on a given investigation and build a team for that particular job. They will also do the same when they do their own investigations. The interviews speak for themselves and hopefully you will find them interesting and thought provoking. There are more locations around the country that I would like to investigate, the problem I now encounter is peoples' greed. It seems that cash is the only key you can use to open doors in supposed haunted locations. I will not investigate somewhere that only reports to be haunted just to rake in money from people with a genuine interest in the paranormal. If someone asks for my help I will do my best to sort out their problem.

I will continue searching the UK for new stories of paranormal activity, and hopefully you will continue to enjoy reading about my exploits.

So until the next time my friends,
Happy Hunting.

Terminology

EVP **Electronic Voice Phenomena**

EMF **Electro Magnetic Field**

RF **Radio Frequency**